WRITING YOUR LIFE

WRITING YOUR LIFE

THE ULTIMATE GUIDE
TO TELLING YOUR STORY

FIRST EDITION

BY ANN HAMER

All stories are used with permission of their authors or authors' heirs: Pamela Applegate, Lynda Barr, Jeanne Behr, Maria C., Barbara Cauthorn, Micki Daniels, Blanca Diaz, Susan Fraizer, Alexandra Gutierrez, Lucerne Hamer, Robert Hamer, Christine Jeston, Joy Karsevar, Luna, M.B., Jeanne Master, Peggy Nelson, Aurora Reinhart, Sallie Ringle, Dorothy Timm Sasine, Ruby Simpson, Rosemary Ventura, and Joan Wallach.

To my mother

Lucerne Hamer

For her unwavering support

and

To all memoir writers

Who tell their stories with courage and love

ACKNOWLEDGEMENTS

My heartfelt thanks goes to all the participants in my writing classes, self-publishing workshops, and writers support groups who have so willingly and openly shared their stories and their friendship. You have taught me so much, and I will always be grateful.

Thanks also to Gibson Senior Center and the City of Upland, California for giving the writing classes a home when we were first starting out.

A heartfelt thanks goes to my proofreaders and editors: Priscilla Fernandez, Samara Gofran, Rick Hamer, Crissie Jeston, Marsha Price, Madison Vlasic, and Joan Wallach. Your feedback and insight has been invaluable.

And finally, a special thanks to Isaiah at Coffee Bean and Tea in Rancho Cucamonga for his feedback on the new cover design, and to my book designer Matthew Morse for his infinite patience and his professional skills.

TABLE OF CONTENTS

FOREWORD

I have always been interested in other people's stories, even when I was very young and visited convalescent hospitals with my Girl Scout troop. Although I was shy and nervous about approaching old people, I still wanted to hear what they had to say. I wanted to hear the stories of my grandparents. I actually *enjoy* looking at other people's vacation photos. I just want to know about *you* and hear your stories.

We all have interesting lives and important stories to tell. What makes our lives so interesting is that they are made up of many parts. Shakespeare said life has seven stages. I'll never be the writer Shakespeare was, but on this point, I beg to differ. There are many, many stages of life - some joyful, some tragic, some boring, or depressing, or fulfilling, or happy. *Writing Your Life: The Ultimate Guide to Telling Your Story* will help you to really *think* about your life. Your story is not just about where you were born, went to school, worked, traveled, and the names of your parents, siblings, spouse, and children. When you explore your feelings and experiences, you come to know what truly makes you the person you are, and this helps the people reading your life story know the real you.

I believe in the power of our stories. You and your life story are important and matter to us all and are a part of our history. The more we write and the more we listen and learn, the more accepting we become of ourselves and of others. Telling your story helps you understand yourself and separate your truths from the myth of family legends and the dry academics of historians. When I listen to the people who take my classes or do the exercises in this book, I am awed by the stories of lives lived with extraordinary bravery, strength, courage, adventure, and humor. When you write your memoir, you are telling the story of the extraordinary person that you truly are.

I invite you to open your heart as you open the pages of this book and write the story of your life.

1

My mother and I were talking about my father shortly after his death in March of 2013. Although she was married to him for many years, and I lived with him for the first 18 years of my life, we both felt that we knew very little about him. He had taken a writing class after he retired, so we had his stories of growing up in Michigan, his military service, his career, and his life after he married and had children. But we knew very little about the inner man - his thoughts and motivations, his dreams, disappointments, hopes, fears, and accomplishments. My father was a private man and revealed little about himself, and now the chance to truly know him was gone.

You and your story are important. You are part of history. Your biography is a written selfie giving a snapshot of your place in time. Your successes and challenges inspire and provide lessons, warnings, encouragement, and hope for generations to come. Memoir writing is not just about your past, it is a way to connect with others and heal for the future.

Welcome to the journey that is your life. As you begin this journey, you may feel overwhelmed. You have just too many memories, too much to write, and not enough time. Writing your autobiography may feel like you're in the Himalayan foothills, staring at the insurmountable obstacle of Mt. Everest, thinking, "I'm going to climb *that*?" Yes you are. Just as you would climb Everest one step at a time and with the help of others, you will use this guide to help you write the story of your life, taking it one step at a time.

Begin by going through this book and selecting a few things to write about. Jot down a few notes as you remember the events and stories of your life. There are no deadlines and you do not need to respond to the writing prompts in order, so take your time. When you go to a restaurant you don't order everything on the menu. Treat this book as the menu for telling your life story. Select a tasty appetizer here, a substantial entrée there and the dessert of a sweet memory.

And then dig in. It's time for you to write the story of your life.

HELPFUL HINT #1
STATE YOUR OBJECTIVES

It's normal to think you have all time in the world to write your memoirs. You may think you're too busy living your life to take the time to write things down. But life happens, and as you learn, grow, and experience, sooner than you expect, days have turned into weeks and weeks have turned into years. So tell your story now and record both your memories and your place in time.

If you find it hard to get started, try creating a list of objectives. When you get stuck, refer to your list to regain your focus and remember why you are writing your story.

Start by writing, "I am writing my memoir because..." Remember, any reasons you have are valid, because this is your story and they are your reasons. There are no right or wrong answers.

Here are some suggestions. You may have others.

- I want to leave a written legacy for my family and friends
- I want my family to know about my life
- I want people to remember me
- I have important things to say and I want to share my wisdom
- I want to help people avoid making the same mistakes I made
- I want to explain my actions
- I want to apologize for hurting others
- I am misunderstood and want people to know the real me
- Lots of interesting things have happened to me
- I want to re-live my past
- I am an interesting person
- I am a nice person
- I am young and I want to write things down so I can look back on my thoughts and experiences as I age
- I am young and I want to use the prompts to help me define my vision and hopes for the future

#1 - CHARACTER SKETCH

Start by writing a two to three page character sketch introducing yourself to your readers

- What is the story you want to tell?

What do you want your memoir to convey about you as a person?

- What are your physical, mental, and emotional characteristics?
- Why does your story need to be told?

What is it essential that people know about you?

- Your values
- Your accomplishments
- Your family
- Places you've seen
- Lessons you've learned
- And?

This is only an outline to help you get started, so you don't need to go into a lot of detail. The details will come later as you respond to the writing prompts in this book.

#2 - WHO ARE YOU?

What is your full name?

- First, last, and middle names

When and where were you born?

- Birth date
- Birth place
- Born in a hospital, at home, in a car, or some other place

What is the story behind your name?

- You're named after someone – family member, family friend, famous person, saint, or religious figure
- Your name was popular when you were born
- Your name represented a special thing, special place, or special event to your parents
- Or?

Did many children in your neighborhood or school have the same first name as you?

Do you feel that your name truly describes *you*?

- If your name doesn't fit, and you could choose another, what would it be?
- Why would this name fit you better than the name you have?

The Origin of My Name

by Alexandra Gutierrez

The day I learned the origin of my real name I was taken aback. My mom told me that my real name is Alejandra. I was named after two of my aunts.

The first aunt was only six when she passed. My grandmother Manula had left her in the care of a relative while she went off to look for work. When she found work in the laundry of the next town, she sent for her daughter. The relative boarded herself and the daughter onto a push-pull cart on the railroad track. As they began their jaunt, a train collided with the cart, and both tragically perished.

At age 19, the second aunt also met with tragedy. She was a young and beautiful girl - full of life and a gifted pianist. Unfortunately, she lived in an era when the pregnancy of an unwed daughter was cause for disgrace. Her parents (my grandparents) met the news with anger and despair. They argued incessantly about how to handle the problem. Should they send her away? Cover-up the pregnancy by having my grandmother wear a pillow under her dress? Or deal with the stigma of having an unwed daughter?

Rather than embrace their daughter's pain, they berated her, and in no uncertain terms let her know what a disappointment she was. In despair, and in the heat of the moment, my aunt picked up a gun, ran down the hill, and shot herself to death.

This aunt, Alejandrina, had taken on the role of nanny to my mom because my grandmother worked all the time while my mother was growing up. When I came along, my mom wanted to name me after her beloved sister Alejandrina, but my grandmother protested vehemently. She argued that she had already lost two daughters with that name. She didn't want to tempt fate with another calamity. After much deliberation, they settled on a compromise, and named me Alejandra, a derivative of Alejandrina.

I like to ponder on how my name came to be. I like to think of how my mom spoke of my aunt with admiration and love, and how she wanted to pass that affection on to me. I like the sound of my name. I think of it as regal. Unfortunately, no one calls me by my real name Alejandra.

Most people call me Sandy. Again, another derivative. Think Alexandra, Andra, Sandra,

Sandy. My immediate family calls me Sandra, my friends call me Sandy, my nieces and nephews call me Aunt Dot, and before I was married, my siblings called me Sister. Who knows???

#3 - NICKNAME

Do you have a nickname?

- How did you get your nickname?

Are you commonly known by your nickname, or is it used only by family and friends?

- Do you like your nickname?

Did you have a childhood nickname?

- Do you still use this nickname?
- Did you like your childhood nickname or was it hurtful or demeaning?

Did you have a different name at home than at school?

- What were you called at home?
- What were you called at school?
- What were you called by your other relatives?

#4 - NAME CALLING

Were you ever called names?

- Sissy
- Bully
- Crybaby
- Tomboy
- Fatty
- Nerd
- Loser
- Stupid
- Ugly
- Or?

How did it make you feel to be called names?

- Does being called names as a child still hurt you or haunt you?

Who called you names?

- Did you ever confront the person who called you names?
- What happened?

Did you ever call other people names?

- Whom did you call names? Why?
- How do you now feel about having called people names when you were a child?

#5 - EARLY

What is your earliest childhood memory?

HELPFUL HINT #2

IT ISN'T WRITING UNTIL YOU WRITE IT DOWN

You aren't writing your memoir if your ideas stay in your head.

Set yourself a goal to write a certain number of pages or for a certain amount of time each day. Jot things down as they come to you. Don't edit, just write. In the beginning don't worry about putting your memories in chronological order. Don't worry about punctuation, spelling, or grammar. Just get your thoughts down. Editing and polishing can come later.

Keep in mind that you do not need to respond to every writing prompt in this book. If a question helps you get started or brings thoughts and memories to mind, then answer it. If a question doesn't apply to you, skip it or come back to it later when it does apply.

Don't let minutia keep you from writing. While it is important to find a comfortable place to write, waiting to wallpaper your writing nook, organize your pens, or buy the latest computer is not the same thing as writing.

You make your autobiography, not finding the perfect piece of pretty paper.

#6 - NEIGHBORHOOD

Visualize the first place you lived and the first neighborhood you remember from your childhood.

What did it look like?

- Urban
- Rural
- Suburban

What features do you remember?

- Your home
- Human-made and natural features
- Your neighbors
- Structures
- Barns and outbuildings
- Geographical features
- Rivers, lakes, ocean
- Scary places
- Where the treasure was buried
- Your favorite hiding place
- Schools
- Stores and manufacturing
- Parks and vacant lots
- And?

Illustrate your visualization by drawing a map or picture.

When you are as detailed as possible with your drawing or map, you remember so much more than just the physical layout of the place. Try to remember specifics such as the closet where the family treasures were kept or the place where the big dog chased you. Your drawing doesn't have to be perfect or beautiful. It just has to be about you.

#7 - CHILDHOOD HOMES

Describe your childhood residence(s)

- House, apartment, farm
- Orphanage, group home, foster home

Describe the community where your home(s) were located

- Urban, rural, suburban
- Desert, beach, mountains, forests, plains
- Special landmarks

Weather

- Four seasons
- Temperate
- Tropical or subtropical

Write as many specific details of your childhood home(s) as you can remember

- Rooms
- Furnishings and décor
- Yard/barn
- Garage or car port
- Attic
- Cellar
- Your favorite room
- Your favorite hiding place

What was stored in the attic, cellar, garage, or outbuilding?

Did you live in the same home while growing up or move around a lot?

- If you moved around a lot, why?

#8 - GROWING UP

Who were the people in your household?

- Father, Mother, siblings
- Grandparents, aunts, uncles, cousins, or other relatives who lived with you
- Non-related household members
- Step-parents
- Step-siblings and half-siblings
- Foster parents

Who were you in the family?

- Oldest child – leader of the pack
- Youngest child – baby
- Only child
- Peacemaker/Gentle Soul
- All Star
- Comedian
- Brat
- Troublemaker
- Mother's helper
- All boy
- Princess/Daddy's girl
- Tomboy
- Or?

What was the role of family members?

- Breadwinner
- Stay-at-home parent
- Bossy older sibling
- Protective brother or sister
- Baby brother or baby sister
- Or?

What activities did you and your family regularly do together?

- Eat meals
- Vacation
- Work in a family business
- Attend worship services
- Share bedtime stories
- Sports and hobbies
- And?

Were you close to your extended family, e.g. grandparents, aunts, uncles, cousins?

- What activities did you do with your extended family?

2617 Euclid Place, Minneapolis 12, Minnesota

by Ruby Simpson

Mom and I moved into the house on Euclid when I was starting second grade. Mom was divorced, so it was just the two of us. She had run away from my father in California to return to her family in Minnesota, and now we were graduating from "the projects" to a real apartment because Mom was making enough money to afford it.

The big brown brick house was gorgeous, settled on a slight rise and just three houses from Lake of the Isles, one of the beautiful lakes in Minneapolis. When we drove up to the house I thought it was the most beautiful place I'd ever seen. We stopped in the porte cochère and were met by Leo Motylewski, our new landlord. He escorted us down the steps from the back door to the basement, turned right down the hall, then left down another hall to the former servants' quarters: one bedroom, a shotgun kitchen, one bathroom, and a living room. There was one small window that peered outside just above the ground. The rent was $50 per month.

It didn't take long for us to move in. The Motylewskis were very hospitable, and we learned that there was another apartment on the second floor of the house, a great big place with a porch and lots of windows. A married couple lived there. Leo and Ardelle and their two daughters, Gale and Charyl, lived in the rest of the 4,700 square foot house. Gail was in eighth grade, Charyl in fifth.

Once we settled in, Mom asked Leo if he knew a good babysitter. She had an active social life and dated a lot, but Leo, knowing money was very tight, said never mind, just send Ruby upstairs. We'll take her whenever you want to go out.

Many evenings Mom would go bowling or on some other date, and I was always welcome at the big kitchen table for dinner. Leo, whom I was soon calling "Daddy", expressed shock at how much I could eat, and accused me of having a hollow leg. After supper we all cleaned up the kitchen and adjourned to the living room to watch "The Walt Disney Show" or "Mighty Mouse" or "Davy Crockett". I was often settled into Daddy's lap. Gale and Charyl were too big by then. Mama Motylewski was on the couch reading, and Gale and Charyl were on the floor in front of the TV, but not too close. Daddy was a big cigar smoker; he smelled of cigars, a lovely masculine smell, and I still love the smell of a good cigar.

Daddy had a workroom in the basement. Besides repairing stuff, he had a big bug collection.

I marveled at those nasty things, but I loved hammering nails into useless pieces of wood and using the plane to make little wood curls. I never tired of sitting on the stool watching him.

After three years, Mom was making enough money to afford a small house in St. Louis Park, and so we moved away. She promised me a puppy which helped a little, but I was inconsolable leaving the house on Euclid Place. I left my autograph book there, so Mommy and Daddy brought it to me at the new house. Inside was inscribed: "To our littlest girl. You will always be our sweet little Ruby and we will always love you."

I didn't see them very often once we moved away, but I stayed in touch by phone and letter. When I married Richard in Washington, DC, Daddy came to my wedding. (Mommy had passed away.) And five years later when I was pregnant with Jennifer and notified him, he sent me the letter I treasure. He wrote, "That little baby is very lucky. You and Richard will make fine parents."

When Richard and I went back to Minneapolis for my cousin's wedding, I took him to 2617 Euclid. Daddy had passed away, and the Motylewski girls had sold the house. I told the nice family who lived there that I'd lived in the basement many years earlier, and they opened the door to welcome Richard and me to their home, and thank God not much had changed. Gosh that basement apartment was tiny!

I hoped that some day when I won the Lotto I could buy that house where I'd been so happy. In fact, it's for sale right now for about $1,800,000. Sadly, the current owners have renovated it to death. It bears hardly any resemblance to the house I knew, and with its coved ceilings and putting green it looks like a fancy house in Brentwood. Never mind about the Lotto. I have the house and the gentle, kind spirits that inhabited it tucked away in my heart.

#9 - IMPORTANT PICTURE

Find a photo of a person or thing important to you.

- Why is this person or thing important to you?

Describe when and where the photo was taken

- What are your memories of that day?

#10 - STORY

What well-known character from children's literature or movies do you most resemble?

- Winnie the Pooh
- Toad of Toad Hall
- Madeline
- The Cat in the Hat
- Tiny Tim
- Bambi or Black Beauty
- One of the "Little Women"
- Nate the Great
- Tom Sawyer or Huck Finn
- A Disney princess
- Ferdinand the Bull
- Lando Calrissian/Han Solo/Princess Leia/Queen Amidala/Yoda
- Katniss Everdeen
- Nancy Drew or one of the Hardy Boys
- Harry Potter/Hermione Granger
- Frodo
- Lemony Snicket
- Alice in Wonderland
- Robinson Crusoe
- Karana from *Island of the Blue Dolphins*
- Dora the Explorer
- Or?

How were you like this character when you were a child?

- Did you ever play the part of this character in your childhood games?

How are you like this character now that you are an adult?

- How are you different?

#11 - FAMILY RESEMBLANCE

How are you similar to your parents and siblings?

- Who do you most resemble in appearance and personality?

How are you different from your parents and siblings?

- Who do you least resemble in appearance and personality?

HELPFUL HINT #3

CHILDHOOD PERSPECTIVES

Remember that children see things differently than adults do. When your parents gave you instructions on how to escape the house in the event of fire, you may not have heard their concern for your safety, but instead reacted with apprehension and fear. As a child, you may have seen only beauty in the stars shining through holes in the roof or when wildflowers bloomed among abandoned cars in the vacant lot near your home.

Try to bring that youthful perspective to your stories when you write about your childhood. Don't describe the past from your current adult perspective, but rather immerse yourself in your past and describe growing up from the viewpoint of the child you once were.

#12 - YOUR PARENTS

What are the full names of your parents?

- Include your mother's maiden name
- Include the names of all people who assumed the parenting role

Were you parented by someone other than your biological father or your biological mother?

- Stepparents
- Foster parents
- Adoptive parents
- Siblings
- Other family members or family friends
- Group home or orphanage

#13 - YOUR PARENTS AT WORK

What did your parents do for employment?

- Did both of your parents work outside of the home?

Did your parents own their own business?

- Did you work in the family business when you were young?
- Were you expected to continue working in the family business as an adult?

Did you have a stay-at-home parent?

- Describe the activities of your stay-at-home parent

Did your family receive any public assistance? Was this assistance long term or temporary?

- Social Security, Medicare, Medicaid, Welfare, Section 8, food stamps, etc.
- Help from a charity

#14 - CHILDHOOD DREAMS

When you were a child, what did you want to do or be when you grew up?

- Why?

Did your childhood dreams come true?

- In what ways did they come true?
- In what ways did they not come true?

If your childhood dreams did not come true, do you still want them to?

- How will you pursue your dreams?

#15 - GIFTS FROM PARENTS

Describe a gift you received from your father, your mother, or both of your parents

- A tangible gift - something special you received
- An intangible gift - a skill or character trait

What values did your parents give you?

- Work ethic
- Religious values
- Love of family
- Loyalty
- Honesty and integrity
- And?

#16 - PARENTAL DISCIPLINE

About what were your parents especially strict?

- Not talking to strangers
- Doing your chores
- Helping in the family business
- Honesty and keeping your word
- Religious beliefs and moral values
- Taking responsibility for your actions
- Doing your schoolwork
- Health and diet
- Money and savings
- Dating and sex
- And?

How did you respond to your parents' attempts to discipline you?

#17 - ACTIVITIES WITH PARENTS

What activities did you do with your parents?

- Parents who were Scout leaders
- Parents who coached sports teams
- Parents who transported you to lessons and after school activities
- Vacations and trips with parents
- Hobbies and interests shared with parents
- Visits to grandparents and other family members
- And?

My Family

by Lucerne Hamer

My mother and father married young. She was seventeen and he was twenty. They both liked to dance, and met and then dated at the ballrooms which were popular in those days. They were married September 26, 1923. They were loving parents, and my brother Frank and I were so very fortunate to be their children. My father worked at his father's business, Sasine & Son Machine Tool and Die Works in Los Angeles. Making movie splicers for Eastman Kodak carried the business through the Depression. During World War II, they made machined aircraft parts for Douglas and North American.

I loved to watch my father's mother make strudel. She would cover the kitchen table with a cloth, and then roll and roll the dough until it was stretched paper thin over the table. I have never eaten strudel to compare with my Grandma's. Grandma and Grandpa S. would also take me to the Turner Club. The adults played cards, ate and talked, almost entirely in German. During World War II Turner Clubs were closed. They were considered subversive.

Thanksgiving was at my Grandma Kennedy's house with turkey and all the fixings. We were a small family so it was just Frank and me, our parents, our grandparents, and our Auntie Ann, my father's sister. Christmas dinner was at the Sasine grandparents. Grandma S. made cookies that were supposedly a favorite of Austrian Emperor Franz Joseph. I was told she had been a cook in one of his palaces, and that was how she got the recipe. I have the recipe and often make the cookies at Christmas. They are a bit tricky and one recipe makes 44 dozen cookies.

In 1938 my mother's mother, Grandma K., bought a lot for my parents in Hermosa Beach. They built a house on the 30x90 foot lot on 17th Street. Except for the time I was at USC, I lived there until I married in 1949. It was a great street. There were children of our ages. We played hide and seek and kick the can. My brother Frank and I were enrolled in swim lessons at the Surf and Sand Club, later the Hermosa Biltmore, which was eventually demolished and replaced with condos. It was a salt water pool and even to this day I cannot get used to a fresh water pool. We became good swimmers. When older, we could go to the beach without a parent, but were never allowed to swim alone. We especially liked to swim in the late afternoon when the waves were larger. I was never very good at catching waves, but it was exciting when I did. Frank surfed with a long hollow wooden paddle board, which he had to stand on its end to drain after each use. I never tried to ride his board because it was way too big for me. Frank was 6'4".

We went to the movies at the local theater a few blocks from home. Our parents liked to sit in the more expensive loge seats because they were more comfortable and had better viewing. There was a double feature, newsreel, cartoon, and sometimes an extra short film. You could come in at any time. After the movie we would walk to the drugstore soda fountain. Father's favorite was a pineapple soda. Of course there were the Saturday kid matinées with the exciting serial and appropriate double feature. Seats were 10 cents and Frank and I got extra money to purchase candy at the store next to the theater. There was no snack bar in the theater.

One summer Mother, Frank, and I went to Pinecrest Resort, near Lake Arrowhead. Father had to work, so he came up weekends during the month we were there. After breakfast I headed for the barn and spent nearly all day riding, grooming, and being around horses. In the evening there were programs, music, dancing, and games in the resort's lounge. It was a fun place and great for families, but it was closed by the time I wanted to take my three children there many years later.

#18 - RELATIONS WITH PARENTS

Did you have a good relationship with your parents?

- Did you have a better relationship with one parent than the other?

What was most enjoyable about your relationship with your parents?

- Shared activities
- Shared humor
- Shared quiet times
- Or?

What did you fight about with your parents?

- How often did you argue?
- What happened as a result of these arguments?

Do you have any unresolved issues with your parents?

- How can you deal with these feelings?
- How will dealing with your feelings change the relationship with your parents?
- If you have unresolved issues with a deceased parent, will dealing with your feelings change the way you remember your parent?

#19 - ABSENT PARENTS

When you were a child, did you lose a parent through either death or divorce?

- How old were you when you experienced this loss?

Do you know what happened?

- The cause of your parent's death
- The reasons for your parents' divorce

Were you required to leave your home or change residences after the loss?

- With whom did you live after the move?
- If your parents divorced, how often did you see your non-custodial parent or did your parents share custody?
- Were you separated from your siblings as a result of the move?

Did your parents remarry?

- Describe your relationships with your stepparents and step and half siblings

#20 - CHANGING WORLD OF HEALTH

When I was a child, if an elderly person fell and broke a hip, it was almost always a death sentence. I used to wonder why, because after all - I thought - it was *just* a broken bone. As I now know, it was not the broken bone that caused the death, but the pneumonia that often resulted from long-term hospitalization and inactivity. Things are different now. When my mom fell and broke her hip, the physical therapist had her up and walking within a day of her surgery.

Did you have a relative or friend who died or was disabled, but due to advances in medical care would probably have survived today?

- Polio
- Infections
- Cancer
- Measles/chicken pox/diphtheria/whooping cough
- Scarlet fever
- Pneumonia
- Tuberculosis
- Small pox
- Broken bones
- Dangers associated with childbirth
- Flu
- HIV / AIDS
- Hepatitis

- Diabetes
- Accident or injury

As you age, how will your health be different from the health of your parents or grandparents?

- Expectation of an active and healthy retirement
- Expectation of a longer life
- And?

#21 - COLOR

Write about a color

- A favorite outfit
- A room
- Food
- Something in nature, e.g. a sunset, a forest, an animal
- An emotion
- A person
- Or?

What color are you?

HELPFUL HINT #4

CHECK IN

At the end of each chapter, take time to check in with yourself. How are you feeling about responding to the prompts and writing your memoirs? Do you enjoy remembering people and events from your past? What about the things you wrote best describes you? What do you want to explore at greater length and in greater depth?

Taking the time to periodically assess your progress will help you focus on the things that are most important to you, and guide you to writing the story you most want to tell.

2

HELPFUL HINT #5

WRITE THE FIRST CHAPTER

Writing the first chapter of your memoir may help you focus on what you want to accomplish. You may want to create a literary legacy for family and friends, use your life story as the basis for a novel, turn your journals into something to share with your family, use this book as a diary to record your current activities and ideas to look at and share in years to come, or preserve your stories for future generations. If you are having a hard time visualizing the structure of your story, writing the first chapter may help you get started.

Begin with a first chapter only if it helps you to start writing. If it freezes you or makes your task seem too overwhelming to even begin, don't do it. Instead, use the writing prompts and Helpful Hints in this book to help you get started and continue with your writing.

The important thing is that you start writing.

#22 - MY MISSION

Write a mission statement that sums up your hopes, goals, and aspirations

Has your mission statement changed or remained the same throughout your life?

- If it has changed, what changes did you make and why?

#23 - MONEY

Describe your attitude toward money

- You can never have enough, and some people call you "money hungry"
- Having enough money for financial security is all you really need; sometimes more than enough is just too much
- You've never had enough money, and that has made life difficult

Have any relationships been ruined because of your attitude toward money?

#24 - TOYS

What were your favorite toys as a child?

- Crayons, paint, clay
- Slinky, Silly Putty, Hula Hoop
- Puzzles
- Cap pistols and BB guns
- Toy soldiers
- Scooters and bikes
- Ice skates and roller skates
- Sleds
- Model building kits
- Tools and hardware
- Electric trains
- Matchbox cars
- Tinker Toys and Erector Sets
- Legos and Lincoln Logs
- Microscopes and chemistry sets
- Animal figurines and models
- Stuffed, plush, or soft toys

- Mini kitchen appliances
- Dolls
- A favorite computer game, interactive game, or app
- And?

#25 - FIRST TOY

Describe the first toy you remember

- Who gave it to you?
- Did you love it?

Do you still have this toy?

- If you don't, what happened to it?

#26 - POCKET MONEY

Did you get an allowance when you were a child?

- How did you earn your allowance?
- What were your regular chores?

Did you have an after school job, part-time job, or earn money online?

- What was your job?
- What did you like about this job?
- What did you dislike about this job?

Did you get cash gifts from family and friends?

- On what occasions did you get cash gifts?

Did your parents give you money when you asked for a "loan"?

- Did you repay this loan?
- If you didn't repay the loan, did your parents forgive the debt?

Did you ever steal money from your mother's purse or your father's wallet?

- Were you ever caught?

How old were you when you stopped asking your parents for money?

#27 - SMILE (1)

What makes you smile?

#28 - SMILE (2)

In the theme song from the old Mary Tyler Moore Show, Mary could, "Turn the world on with her smile."

What does your smile do for the world?

#29 - HUMOR

What is

- The funniest thing you ever said?
- The funniest thing you ever heard?
- The funniest thing you ever saw?
- Your favorite joke?
- The joke you tell to everyone?

#30 - BELLY LAUGH

Write about a time when you heard someone you love *truly* laugh out loud

- What was so funny?
- Did you laugh too?

How did it make you feel to hear your loved one laugh out loud?

#31 - YOUR FATHER

Use this prompt to write about any person in the fathering role, e.g. step-father, sibling, foster parent, or guardian.

How are you like your father?

- How are you unlike your father?

What do you love or admire most about your father?

- What do you least admire or dislike about your father?

How did your father influence you?

#32 - YOUR MOTHER

Use this prompt to write about any person in the mothering role, e.g. step-mother, sibling, foster parent, or guardian.

How are you like your mother?

- How are you unlike your mother?

What do you love or admire most about your mother?

- What do you least admire or dislike about your mother?

How did your mother influence you?

Scrabble

by Ann Hamer

At least three times a week Mom and I go out for lunch and Scrabble. Sometimes we buy our lunch, going to places like Legends where there's always enough left over for dinner, and sometimes we take our lunch to the patio on 19th Street outside Starbucks and the Verizon Store. I get a soda from Jersey Mike's and we eat hard boiled eggs and peanut butter sandwiches from home.

Mom and I are getting way too clever at Scrabble for our own good. We maneuver away from setting each other up for a triple word score, especially if the Q, Z, or J have not yet played, and end up boxing ourselves into corners where the only possible play is a two letter word or something like "toe" or "the". Often I get exasperated by the tight corners and play into uncharted territory. Mom then pounces, playing "quiz" on a triple word score. The fierceness of my kind and gentle mom when given the chance for a big score is truly amazing. No holds are barred in Scrabble.

At least once every game I play a word I know is a word, but being the queen of insecurity that I am, I look it up in the Scrabble Dictionary anyway. The Scrabble Dictionary is not exactly Merriam Webster's Unabridged, so definitions are sketchy and frankly - kind of odd. Sometimes when I look up something and read a definition, I'll say to Mom, "Really - who knew?" Qi is the same as ki. Both mean life force, not to be confused with gi which is a garment worn in martial arts. All handy Scrabble words to know, especially near the end of the game.

The other day I looked up "pied". I know pied is a word. It means multi-colored like the

Pied Piper and his patchwork coat, or the Pie with his mottled markings in *National Velvet*. That's not the definition in the Scrabble Dictionary. When I read it, I started laughing.

"What?" asked Mom.

"Do you know what 'pied' means according to Scrabble?"

Mom shook her head.

I read from the Dictionary, "Pied - the past tense of pie."

Neither of us even knew that pie was a verb. How do you go about pie-ing someone? What is the meaning of "to pie"?

There are some words that are both nouns and verbs. You go on a vacation (noun), but when you're there, you're vacationing (verb). You make toast by toasting bread.

But to pie?

Do actors in old slapstick comedies pie each other when they smash custard into one another's face? If you paint something many and varied colors, are you pie-ing a wall? If you put a quart of fruit into a crust, are you pie-ing blueberries?

I suppose it's possible that the person in charge of the "P" section of the Scrabble Dictionary had never heard of the Pied Piper or *National Velvet*, but if she had looked up "pied" on her omni-present iPhone as I did, the first definition of "pied" is multi-colored. I know there are words I've never heard of in the Scrabble Dictionary - "chillax" and "geocache" for example - and when I scrolled down, according to the Urban Dictionary, "pied" means ignoring someone or not returning a high five. Who knew? Cool, rad, and groovy, I say. My playing "pied" became meaningless anyway.

Mom played "zax" (a tool for trimming roof slates) on a triple word score, and blasted by me, winning the game.

I think I was pied.

But I was a gracious loser. How very chillax of me.

#33 - WATCHING

Go to a public place - a mall or park, your local coffee place, an airport, or train station and sit for a while watching people.

Write a story about a person you watched

What is it about this person that caught your eye?

- Why are they there?
- What are they doing?

Is there anything about this person that reminds you of yourself?

#34 - PARENTAL ADVICE

What are the things your mother and father always said to you?

- Did you consider these "words of wisdom" or something to be ignored?

What are the things your parents said to you that you swore you'd never say to your own children?

- Do you say these things to your children and grandchildren anyway?

Does your parents' advice seem wiser to you now that you are an adult?

#35 - SIBLINGS

What are the full names of your siblings?

- Brothers
- Sisters
- Half-siblings and step-siblings

Were you close to your siblings when you were growing up?

- Were you close in age?
- What activities did you do together when you were children?

Did you argue with your siblings?

- Describe a fight you had
- What did you fight about?
- What happened as a result of this fight?

Are you close to your siblings now?

- What activities do you do together?
- What do you fight about?

If you are estranged from any sibling, what caused the estrangement?

- When did you start to grow apart?
- Is there a chance of reconciliation?

Which sibling are you most like?

- Why?

Which sibling are you least like?

- Why?

How did your siblings influence you?

- As a child
- As a teen
- As a young adult
- Now

#36 - BIRTH CERTIFICATE

If you were adopted, your original birth certificate may have been sealed prior to your adoption.

If you have seen your original birth certificate, did it reveal things that you did not know about yourself or your family?

- Your original birth name was different
- You discovered the names of your biological parents

Have you contacted any biological relatives you discovered as a result of finding your birth certificate?

- Were your biological relatives glad to hear from you?
- How did your biological relatives respond when they heard from you?
- Will you maintain a relationship with your biological relatives?

How did your adoptive family react when you made contact with your biological family?

- Were they supportive?
- Were they hurt?
- Did they want to meet your biological relatives?

HELPFUL HINT #6

BE READY TO WRITE

Keep pen and paper or your electronic device close by so you can write your thoughts and memories as they occur to you. When you go for a walk take along something to record your thoughts. It's easy to tell yourself you will remember something, and just as easy to forget. By keeping pen and paper handy, you will be able to make a note of things as the books you read or the shows you watch or the things you see waken your memories and remind you of events from your past.

#37 - GAMES KIDS PLAY

What games did you play as a child?

- Kick the can
- Hide and seek
- Sandbox
- Horses
- Dungeons and Dragons
- House
- Board games and card games
- Cowboys and the "Wild West"
- Combat and war
- Holiday games
- Dodgeball, "four square", tetherball
- Games based on TV shows or movies
- Games based on historical or fictional characters
- Astronaut or space explorer
- Spy
- Magician or wizard
- Interactive online games
- Game-boy and video games
- And?

What games did you play as a child that you still play?

What games did you play as a child that you'd like to play again?

- Will you?

#38 - AND THE WINNER IS

When you feel stuck and can't seem to move ahead with your memoir, try writing something fanciful and perhaps even a little bit silly. Sprinkled throughout this guide you will find prompts that are designed to help you do just that. Here is the first of these fun prompts.

If you could give yourself an award or prize what would it be?

- Nobel prize
- Academy award
- Grammy or CMA
- Edgar, Agatha, Anthony, or Hugo
- Pulitzer
- Emmy
- Scouting badge
- Olympic medal
- Heisman Trophy
- Tony or Obie
- Mother or Father of the year
- Employee of the month
- Or?

What do you imagine yourself doing to win this award?

Write your acceptance speech

#39 - CHILDHOOD READING

What books did you read and love as a child and teen?

- Do you ever re-read these books as an adult?
- Do you still love them?

#40 - READING

When I get a little money I buy books, and if there is any left I buy food and clothes.

- DESIDERIUS ERASMUS -

Do you read for pleasure?

- What types of books do you read?
- If you don't read for pleasure, why not?

Are there any issues that make reading difficult for you, e.g. dyslexia?

- Were these issues diagnosed and treated when you were a child?
- If they went undiagnosed, when were you finally diagnosed and treated?
- How did this impact your school experience?

#41 - UNIFORM

Write about a time you wore a uniform

- School
- Girl Scouts or Boy Scouts
- Military service
- For a job
- Or?

HELPFUL HINT #7

FINDING YOUR VOICE

You may need to do a lot of writing in order to find your authentic voice. If you are an attorney, a scientist, an engineer, or in a highly technical profession with a lot of specialized language and forms of communication, you may need to write a lot before you get that overly formal or concise tone out of your writing. Keep on writing and responding to the prompts in this book until you are able to give voice to the real you.

#42 - RUN AWAY (1)

Did you ever run away from home when you were a child?

- How old were you the first time you ran away?

What made you decide to run away the first time?

- Did you run away more than once?

How did you prepare to run away?

- Packed food and took money
- Wrote a note
- Told a friend or trusted adult
- Mapped your route
- Or?

How were you treated when you returned home?

#43 - SCARY

The passage that had to be negotiated was interminably long and lit only by an oil lamp at its far end. This was an awful place, for under a marble slab in its dim recesses, a stuffed crocodile reposed. In the daytime the crocodile PRETENDED to be very dead, but everyone knew that as soon as it grew dark, the crocodile came to life, and padded about the passage on its scaly paws seeking for its prey, with its great cruel jaws snapping, its fierce teeth gleaming, and its horny tail lashing savagely from side to side. It was common knowledge that the favorite article of diet of crocodiles was a little boy with bare legs in a white sailor suit.

- F R E D E R I C K   S P E N C E R   H A M I L T O N -

What things scared you when you were a child?

- The dark
- Thunder and lightning
- Water or drowning
- Dogs
- Wild animals
- Bugs or spiders

- The neighborhood "haunted" house
- Heights
- Locked rooms
- The "boogie man"
- Bad dreams
- The scary place your parents told you not to go
- Earthquakes, floods, other natural disasters
- War or "the bomb"
- Being physically hurt
- Violence, guns, mass shootings
- Ghosts
- Aliens, trolls, monsters, gnomes
- Something under your bed
- Strangers
- Speaking in front of your class at school
- Or?

What gave you the idea that this thing was scary?

- Something a parent or sibling said to you
- Something a friend told you or that "everyone" knew
- It was dark or hard to see
- You misunderstood something said to you

How did you deal with your fear?

- Faced it as bravely as you could
- Ran away
- Closed your eyes
- Held your breath
- Made a wish
- Talked to a family member
- Slept with your parents or a sibling
- Said a prayer or called on angels
- Tried to ignore it
- Or?

How did you overcome your fear?

#44 - YOUR GRANDPARENTS

Who were your grandparents?

- Their names, including maiden names of your grandmothers
- Their birth dates and birth places
- If your grandparents are deceased, when and where they died, and where they are buried

What did you call your grandparents?

- What did your grandparents call you?

What are the stories of your grandparents?

- Stories they told you about their youth and young adulthood
- How your grandparents met and married

Did your grandparents find any of their stories painful, shameful, or difficult to share?

- What were these painful stories?
- How did you learn of these stories?

How did your grandparents influence you?

#45 - FAMILY STORIES AND LEGENDS

My family knows very little about my paternal grandmother. We know where she was born and where she grew up. We know her formal education ended with the eighth grade. We know she was one of ten children, only five of whom lived to maturity. We know when she married and the names of her children. But we know almost nothing about what made her the person she was. We don't know why she was a voracious reader until the day she died. We don't know why she left the farm in Michigan where she was raised. We know very little about her life before becoming a wife and mother. And now that she and her children are deceased, her stories are lost forever.

What are the family stories and legends you want to preserve that may be lost forever if you do not record them now?

- What stories did your parents, grandparents, and great-grandparents tell you about their lives?

Grandfather Santiago - The Pot of Gold in San Quentin

by Maria C.

Santiago was my paternal grandfather. To his grandchildren he was our "Apong Ago." Ago is a short name for his full name, and Apong in Pampango (the Philippine dialect he spoke) means grandfather.

My grandfather came from a humble family. His parents must have been farmers since he grew up in Pampanga, and this region of the Philippines is known for its rice fields. I remember him saying they used to catch frogs in the rice fields and bring them home for dinner. I don't know how he met my grandmother, but I am pretty sure they grew up in the same town. I recall him saying he met my grandmother at a young age.

In his early married life my grandfather was a farmer. However, he was not content with his lot. He knew he could do better. Grandfather took a chance and ventured into the buying and selling of goods. He became a *viajero*. The word *viajero* is a Spanish word; colloquially it means traveling salesman.

Apong Ago would go by train or bus to remote towns of Pangasinan province. He supplied local markets with various dry goods such as blankets, towels, clothing, shoes, slippers, and other basic needs. He had a good head for business and knew his market. His business flourished, and he hired a crew of *viajeros* to help him meet growing demand.

One of the towns Grandfather visited was San Quentin. He saw the rice fields there were more affordable than in his own hometown. Grandfather bought several hectares of rice fields. San Quentin turned out to be his gold mine. From an ordinary farmer, my grandfather turned his life around and became a wealthy landowner, well beyond his imagination.

Through this vast property, he was able to support his family in a lifestyle he had not enjoyed. Apong Ago's hard work and investments paid off. My grandfather paid for my dad's medical school and then sent him to post-graduate studies at Columbia University in New York. During those days, only the old rich and established families could send their children to study abroad. There were no scholarships or government assistance. Indeed, my grandfather "leap-frogged" to a new social status.

When I was in high school, Grandfather suffered a stroke. He was paralyzed and had slurred speech. After his stroke he completely withdrew from the world. Most of the time Apong Ago had a blank stare, and didn't talk much. Certainly a far cry from the tough, confident, intense grandfather I knew growing up.

One summer evening in May 1974, my sisters Josie and Cita, cousins Alice and Lettie, and I decided to visit our grandfather. We were just back from a bridal shower, and it seemed like a good time to drop by. When we got there, his caregiver was spoon feeding him a bowl of chicken rice soup. It was pitiful to see Grandfather in that state. In his younger years, Apong Ago was known for his huge appetite. His table spread would be a five course meal, with soup, entrees of his favorite beef, pork, chicken, fish, and finally a rich dessert. Now, my poor grandfather could not even finish a bowl of bland soup.

We circled around, cheering him on to finish his soup. Even with our positive vibes and enthusiasm, there was no reaction from my grandfather. It was just his normal blank stare. Since this was a depressing scene for us, we decided not to stay long. Our grandfather didn't say a word, but we all noticed tears rolling down his cheeks. He looked extremely sorrowful, and he was peering intently at each one of us. We thought nothing much of this incident when we left the house.

The moment my sisters and I got back to our parents' house, my mother got a call. My grandfather had passed away. We thought this was not possible since we had seen him less than an hour before. Our beloved grandfather died while we were on our way home. He must have sensed death was coming, and cried because he was leaving us. Apong Ago died that fateful evening of May 15, 1974.

Grandfather Santiago gave us a bright future. Our family and the present generation would not be where we are now if not for his vision, hard work, and the tremendous sacrifices he made in his early years. Apong Ago's investments and good fortune all trickled down to our generation.

Thank you, dear Grandfather Santiago, your life story is indeed an inspiration to all of us, and rightfully deserves to be told to your great-grandchildren and great-great-grandchildren.

I love you my dear grandfather, Apong Ago!

#46 - MISCONCEPTIONS

What misconceptions did you have as a child?

- Due to misinformation, e.g. where babies came from
- Due to something you misheard

How did you discover the truth?

- How did you feel when you discovered the truth?
- How old were you?

#47 - DNA

Have you found relatives previously unknown to you as a result of having your DNA tested?

- Who are they?
- How are they related to you?

How did you make your first contact?

- Phone, email, regular mail, through an intermediary
- How did your relatives react when they heard from you for the first time?

Have you had a face-to-face meeting with these previously unknown relatives?

- How did you feel when you met them for the first time?
- Have you established relationships?
- If you have not yet met in person, will you?

Did you discover an ethnicity you did not know you had as a result of your DNA test?

- How will you explore this new discovery?

#48 - YOUR GENERATION

What is your generation?

- The "Greatest Generation"
- Beat Generation
- Baby Boomers
- Gen X
- Millennials
- Or?

What were the most important issues to members of your generation?

- Employment and economic security
- Military service
- Social protest
- Equality and equal opportunity
- Civil rights
- The environment
- Religion
- The drug culture
- Politics
- Technology
- Personal safety
- Or?

How does being a member of this generation define you?

- What do you have in common with other members of your generation?
- How are you different from other members of your generation?

What things do you like about the members of your generation?

- What things do you dislike about the members of your generation?

#49 - TECHNOLOGY

Did you grow up with technology or need to adapt to it?

- Smart phones
- Online gaming
- Computers and tablets
- Social media
- Netflix

If you had to adapt to technology, how did you handle it?

- Just fine, you like the challenge of learning new things
- Kicking and screaming all the way

How do you currently use technology?

#50 - REMEMBER WHEN

Do you remember

- When "computers" fulfilled your foreign language requirement in school
- Having to show your work in math class
- Drop drills
- Cars with bench seats and manual transmissions
- When air conditioning was an option
- Rotary dial telephones anchored to the wall
- When teachers used chalk boards and overhead projectors
- Pocket protectors and slide rules
- White wall tires, curb feelers, "wind wings", and hand crank car windows
- "Girl's bikes"
- Mimeograph and microfiche machines and typewriters
- "Help Wanted Male" and "Help Wanted Female" ads in the newspaper
- Dress codes in school
- And?

HELPFUL HINT #8

BE PERSISTENT

Writing is all about persistence. You will not move forward with your project if you just stand still. You have to be willing to fail, because only by being willing to fail, will you be willing to put in the effort needed for success. Take some encouragement from the inventor Thomas Alva Edison who said, "I have not failed. I've just found 10,000 ways that don't work." And then he continued trying. And so can you.

#51 - BLACK SHEEP

Who are the most infamous or villainous members of your family?

- What did they do to earn their reputation?

Do you know their side of the story?

#52 - FAMILY MYSTERIES

What are the unresolved mysteries in your family?

- A mysterious disappearance
- An unexplained death or suicide
- Abnormal behavior or mental illness
- An unexpected birth
- Or?

What do family members believe are the explanations for these mysteries?

- What do you believe?

#53 - ODDEST

Describe your oddest or most eccentric relative

#54 - TROUBLE

Describe the most trouble you've ever been in

- As a child
- As a teen
- As an adult

What did you do to get in trouble?

- Why did you do it?

What was the outcome?

- You were caught and punished
- You got away with it

#55 - OLD FOLKS

Who was the oldest member of your family when you were a child?

What was the status of this person in your family?

- Revered and respected for wisdom gained from a long life
- Discounted and forgotten as being too old to matter

What is the story of this person?

- Name
- Birth date and birth place
- When and where this person died and is buried

What stories did this person tell you about their youth and young adulthood?

What are your memories of this person?

- Were there any special things just the two of you did together?

Da

by Christine Jeston

The oldest member of my family when I was growing up was my mother's father. George Boreham McLeod was born in Edinburgh, Scotland in 1879. We called him Da. His father, Robert McLeod, was an interior decorator who mixed his own paints and was well known in Edinburgh and Glasgow for his colors. His family was not very well off due to his excessive drinking. I suppose that had an influence on Da's life as he never drank alcohol. He was also a pacifist and a socialist when he grew up.

When Da was a young boy he learned to box, and one day some bullies jumped him. A postman saw Da had the upper hand, so he held him down, and the other boys kicked him so badly that his woolen sock became embedded in one of his legs. He was afraid to tell his parents, and so his leg never healed properly. He suffered all his life because of it. Doctors wanted to amputate Da's leg, but my grandma had heard of a German doctor in Sydney and decided to take Da to see him. The doctor saved his leg by putting Fuller's Earth on it. It was something Da did every day of his life, and then wrapped clean bandages around the leg. I was horrified when I spied his leg one day as it looked to me like very thin almost transparent skin stretched over black and blue flesh and bone. The image has never left me.

The house at 13 Ethel Street Vaucluse where Ma and Da lived had a glasshouse out the back. It was full of boxes of tiny colored glass which threw off many colors and wonderful patterns when the sun shone through them. It was so magical and I just loved that little house. Sometimes Da would forage around in there for hours moving the glass around not saying anything, but I would be at his heels watching him. He had the largest lead light business in Sydney during the 1920s and 1930s. They were very well off and lived in a big house. He made beautiful stained glass windows, doors, and chandeliers that hung in some very prominent homes and famous buildings. Da lost the business during the Depression. He didn't work again until my mother started her own business ten years later and employed Ma and Da so they would have some income.

When we moved to the house in Waverley, Da would walk there from Vaucluse most days to have a cup of tea with my mother, and then walk back again. It was more than 20 miles each way, and it would take him all day. He would sometimes catch a bus for part of the way, and would often sit on the benches at the bus stops to rest. He had a habit of sleeping with his mouth and eyes open, and it was no surprise when one day Mum got a phone call from the local police to say Da had passed away at a bus stop. My mother was shocked when she went down to identify him, and found him sitting up drinking a cup of tea and eating a biscuit. This happened several times, and on one occasion when my dad took the call from a policeman he asked, "Are you sure? The old bugger has a habit of coming back." Dad was right. Da was just sleeping again.

I liked the way Da was interested in people and often stopped to talk to neighbors, admiring their gardens and asking after their families. Everyone had a soft spot for him. I think he spoke to other people more than he spoke to any of us. He had the ability to just be. He loved to stop and listen to the ocean crash against the rocks at the bluff. He enjoyed walks in Waverley Cemetery looking at the headstones of famous people. He would just take in the day. He never had a bad word to say about anyone. I certainly admired his tolerance and peace. He didn't seem to hold on to anything. He was OK with how things were, whether good or bad. He always knew it would work out. I think you learn a lot in 90 years. One thing I remember him saying was, "No one can ever hurt you unless you let them." That has always stuck with me.

Da had a brass bell that looked like Queen Victoria, and would ring it when he was ready for his tea. I still have his brass bell on my shelf and I wouldn't let it go for anything.

#56 - FAMILY STRENGTH

Who is the strongest person in your family?

- How does this person demonstrate their strength?

How are you like this person?

#57 - OLD CLOTHES

Clothes make the man. Naked people have little or no influence on society.

- MARK TWAIN -

Do you have any old clothes you just can't seem to give up?

- What is it about this piece of clothing that you love?
- Do you still wear it?

#58 - EMBARRASSMENT

Describe your most embarrassing moment

- As a child
- As a teen
- As an adult
- Recently

#59 - BAD DREAM

Write about a bad dream you remember

- From your childhood
- From your adulthood
- Recently

Do you have any recurring bad dreams?

- What do you think your bad dreams are trying to tell you?

#60 - COMING TO AMERICA

Use this prompt to tell the stories of you or your family's immigration, even if the destination was not the United States.

How and why did your family come to the United States?

- Where were your parents, grandparents, and great-grandparents born?
- If they were born outside the US, why did they immigrate?
- Was your family name changed to make it more "Western" or easier for Americans to pronounce?

How did you and your family end up living where you live now?

- If you were the only one to immigrate, what led you to make this decision?
- Why did the rest of your family choose to stay in the "old country"?

If your parents or other family members did not immigrate or settle near you

- How often do you see them?
- Where do you meet?
- How do you stay in touch?
- What family events and milestones have you missed?

What was the first thing you noticed about your new home that was different from the home you left behind?

- What things surprised you the most about your new home?
- What things disappointed you about your new home?

What thing(s) did you bring with you to remind you of your old home?

#61 - GOING BACK

Have you ever visited the home of your ancestors?

- What was the experience like?
- Did you feel any sense of homecoming?
- Do you have any desire to live there?

Did you meet any relatives living there?

- Was this a new relationship, or were you re-establishing old relationships?
- Will you maintain contact with these relatives?

#62 - LANGUAGE

What languages were spoken in your home when you were a child?

If your parents spoke a non-English language, did you to learn to speak this language?

- If not, why not?

What languages do you speak now?

- Did you teach your own children to speak the language of their heritage?

HELPFUL HINT #9
IT'S NOT A HISTORY LESSON

No one likes a know-it-all, so don't lecture and don't use your memoir to display your knowledge of history. Insert a few facts to set the scene, but don't go overboard. Stating that your family moved to the farm after your father lost his job during the Great Depression is enough. You do not need to overwhelm your readers with pages of dispassionate facts and economic theory.

Use history to help establish context. Remember that you are writing the story of your life and not a textbook, so don't bog down your narrative with historical detail. When you keep the narrative lively, your readers will become involved in your story and continue turning the page.

#63 - HISTORY

Describe any actions taken by you or your family in response to historical events or social trends

- Economic downturn or depression
- War
- Changes in government
- Epidemic
- Natural disaster
- Economic upturn or boom
- The Space Race
- The Jazz Age/Roaring Twenties
- Terrorism
- Shift in population from farm to city
- The technological age
- Mass shootings
- Or?

#64 - SPECIAL DAY

Tell the story of a special day in your life

- A special birthday
- The day you fell in love
- Your wedding day
- Birth of a child or grandchild
- Graduation
- A day during an important trip
- The first day of a job
- The most beautiful sight you've seen
- The best meal you ate
- The first time
- Your first day at school or university
- A day you survived danger
- A day you received a difficult diagnosis
- A day you triumphed
- Your luckiest day

#65 - HOLIDAY TRADITIONS

Describe your family's holiday traditions

- What food is eaten, who is invited, where are celebrations held, what is done to celebrate?
- Special songs, games, music, decorations, readings

Do your celebrations blend traditions from more than one culture?

How have holiday celebrations changed from your childhood family to your adult family?

- What holidays did you celebrate as a child that you no longer celebrate?

What holiday traditions did you create?

- Family traditions you changed and adapted as an adult
- Traditions that are a blending of your childhood family's traditions and the family traditions of your spouse or partner
- New traditions you adopted from the celebrations of friends

#66 - HOLIDAYS

Describe the best holiday you ever had

Describe the worst holiday you ever had

#67 - HOLIDAY LETTER

Many people send holiday letters summing up the year's events. The story of your life is not just about what happened years ago, it is also about what is happening now. Even if you do not mail this letter, it's a good way to look back on the year and record recent events in your life.

Write a holiday letter

- Describe what you did during the past year: people and places visited, illness survived, successes at work and school, birth and loss, new things you tried, plays you saw, books you read, meals you ate, jobs you undertook, elections and awards you won, and anything else that made up the fabric of your life during the year

#68 - YEAR END (1)

How do you feel when one year ends and a new year begins?

- Is there a customary way that you "ring out the old" and "ring in the new"?

Do you make New Year's resolutions?

- Do you follow through with your resolutions, or usually give up a few weeks into the new year?

What are your usual resolutions?

- Lose weight
- Quit smoking
- Quit drinking/drugs
- Exercise
- Save money
- Get a new job
- Fall in love
- Develop a new skill
- Improve proficiency in something you already know how to do
- Travel
- Or?

#69 - YEAR END (2)

What does the end of the year mean to you?

- Holidays
- Returning to school in the fall
- College football
- Final exams
- The changing of seasons
- Remembering past holidays
- The first New Year after the loss of a loved one
- Fall and winter activities - skiing, ice skating, shoveling snow (or summer activities if you live in the Southern Hemisphere)
- Or?

3

HELPFUL HINT #10

MAKE A COMMITMENT

Make a commitment to write every day. Even if you manage only a few words, at least once a day take up your pen or sit at your computer and write.

When you don't feel like doing any of the exercises in this book, try making lists, posting on social media, or writing a letter. It will help you to complete your memoir if you get into the habit of writing.

#70 - DINNER PARTY

Describe your ideal dinner party

- A perfect dinner party you hosted
- A perfect dinner party you attended
- The fantasy dinner party you would like to host
- The fantasy dinner party you would like to attend

Who was there?

- What food was served?
- When and where was it held?
- What topics were discussed?

What made it so perfect?

#71 - BIRTHDAYS

Rather than adding more and more candles to your birthday cake as you age, consider this suggestion from a friend. Use only three candles: one for the past, one for the present, and one for the future. I love this idea, and now celebrate my own birthday using only three candles.

Write a birthday message

- This does not have to be a message you plan to send to someone

Here are some suggestions

- To a friend or family member about a birthday you celebrated or plan to celebrate
- To yourself about a birthday that was either celebrated or not celebrated in a way you wanted or anticipated
- Birthday wishes to someone special in your life
- Birthday wishes to someone you haven't said "Happy Birthday" to in a long time
- Birthday wishes to a deceased loved one

#72 - YOUR BIRTHDAY

Describe your most memorable birthday

- The best birthday you ever had
- The worst birthday you ever had

Describe your recollections of "milestone" birthdays

- 16th, 18th, 21st, 40th, 50th, 65th, 75th ...
- Bar or Bat Mitzvah
- *Quinceañera*
- Or?

What significance did these milestone birthdays have for you?

- Did you experience any important transitions or new responsibilities associated with these milestones?
- How did these transitions impact you?

Here are some suggestions

- Your first birthday party
- A birthday when you received the gift you always wanted
- A birthday when you received a disappointing gift
- A birthday that was either celebrated or not celebrated in a way you wanted or anticipated
- A time your birthday was forgotten or you were alone
- A time you were surprised

How has the way you celebrate your birthday changed as you've aged?

#73 - MOTHER'S DAY / FATHER'S DAY

What is the favorite Mother's Day or Father's Day gift

- You ever gave?
- You ever received?

Is there a sentiment you wish you had expressed to your parent on Mother's Day or Father's Day?

- What do you want to say?
- To whom do you want to say it?
- What prevented you from expressing these sentiments?

What Mother's Day or Father's Day gift do you wish you had received?

- From whom do you wish you had received it?

My Mother

by Dorothy Timm Sasine
Mother's Day, 1944

I've looked the field all over, on
this bright Mother's day -
To find a card that means just
what I'd like to say -
The thoughts are sentimental, and
every word is true -
But in my estimation, just not good
enough for you.

I think back to the yesterdays, and
the many things you've done -
The many times I worried you, and
kept you on the run -
I didn't think about it then, but I
certainly do now -
Your love was always with me,
you understood somehow.

Today you haven't changed, you're still
so good and fine -
Tomorrow you'll be just the same,
growing dearer with time -
My love is with you always, not just
one day a year -

To me each day is your own day,
God Bless You Mother Dear.

#74 - CAKE

Celebrations and happy occasions often involve cake. Think of weddings and birthdays, a cake traditional in your family for holidays and special occasions, or the cake you entered in a competition.

Write about your favorite cake

- The first cake you baked by yourself
- A special cake you baked with a relative or friend
- A traditional cake with a recipe passed through your family from generation to generation
- The best cake you ever made
- The best cake you ever tasted
- A prize-winning cake
- The cake you always have or make for holidays and special occasions
- The cake you always have for your birthday
- The cake you had for a special celebration, e.g. a wedding cake
- A cake you had on a special vacation or trip
- A cake that didn't turn out quite right
- Or?

#75 - SPECIAL FOOD

What special recipes, meals, or foods do you and your family have for celebrations and special occasions?

- As a child?
- As an adult?

What are the family stories or traditions associated with these recipes?

- Family recipes handed down from generation to generation
- A dish always served on special occasions or holidays

Who taught you how to make these special foods?

- What are your memories of learning to make these foods?
- Have you taught these special recipes to your children and grandchildren?

Describe the recipes

- Ingredients and directions

#76 - COOKING

Describe the first thing you learned to cook

- Who taught you?
- How old were you?
- How did it turn out?

#77 - FAVORITE FOOD

What was your favorite food as a child?

- Who prepared it?
- How often was it prepared?

What was your favorite food made by the person who raised you?

- What was your least favorite food made by the person who raised you?

#78 - CHILDHOOD HEALTH

What diseases, illnesses, or serious accidents did you experience as a child?

- Were you ever hospitalized?
- What led to your hospitalization?

What impact did your illnesses and accidents have on you and your family?

- Were there any aftereffects that continue to impact your life?

Did you have a sibling or parent who had a serious accident or illness when you were a child?

- How did the ill health of your sibling or parent impact you and the rest of your family?

#79 - CURES

Have you invented any home cures for medical conditions?

- Have you taught your home cures to other family members?

Have you treated your children or grandchildren with your home cures?

- Were they healed after receiving your home cures?

Have any old family cures or traditional folk medicine cures worked for you?

- Describe these cures
- Were you given these cures as a child?
- Do you still use these cures?

HELPFUL HINT #11

SOME TIPS TO HELP YOU REMEMBER

- Gather together photos, diaries, journals, scrapbooks, school yearbooks, and public records such as birth, marriage, and death certificates.
- Talk to family and friends, but remember your memory of an event may not be the same as theirs. Conversations may help you remember, but try not to let them influence your memory of events. This is your story. Try to be accurate, but you don't need to be "fair". If others disagree with you, they can write their own memoir!
- Unpack closets and boxes and take out the things you have saved. You kept these things for a reason and now is the time to tell their story.
- Play the music of your past. A song may jog your memory.
- Look through history books for photos that remind you of where you were and what you were doing at a particular time. The photo of a historical event may remind you of a personal experience that has nothing to do with the event itself.
- If you are stuck, take a break. Go for a walk, have a snack, phone a friend. Remember this is not school, and there are no due dates or deadlines.

#80 - SCHOOL DAYS

When and where did you go to school?

- Pre-school
- Elementary school
- Middle school or junior high
- High school
- Trade school

- Public school or private school
- Non-traditional or online school
- Home schooling

What did your school look like?

- How many students were in your class and in your school?

Did you walk to school, take a bus, or get taken to school by a parent or other adult?

- Did you walk to school alone, with siblings, or with other kids from your neighborhood?

#81 - YOUR STUDIES

Were you a good student?

- What were your favorite and least favorite subjects?

What special awards and honors did you receive?

- Academic awards and scholarships
- Sports awards
- Good citizenship awards
- Or?

#82 - SCHOOL FADS

What were the fads when you were in school?

- Clothes and jewelry
- Hair styles
- Music
- TV shows and movies
- Toys and games
- Sports
- After school activities
- Apps and online games
- And?

What did you wear to school?

- Were you allowed to chose your own school clothes?
- Did you get new school clothes in the fall?
- Was there a dress code or school uniform?

#83 - SCHOOL ACTIVITIES

What were your extra-curricular activities?

- Athlete or cheerleader
- School government
- School and non-school clubs
- Field trips
- Class monitor ("chalkboards", "windows", "keys")
- Drama, band, glee club
- And?

Describe your social life

- Dating and romance
- First boyfriend/girlfriend
- First kiss
- Dances
- And?

HELPFUL HINT #12

CREATE A CAST OF CHARACTERS

Be sure to include a "Cast of Characters" with your memoir. Include the relationship of each person to you as the narrator. The people well-known to you and your children may be unknown to future generations, so it is important to include this information with your memoir.

See Appendix #6 for a sample Cast of Characters.

#84 - FAVORITE SCHOOL DAYS

What were your favorite school days?

- First day of school
- Holiday celebrations

- Sporting events
- Elections
- Homecoming, prom, other school dances
- A favorite class
- Special days that were part of your school's own traditions
- The last day of school before vacation

#85 - TROUBLE AT SCHOOL

Did you get in trouble at school?

- What did you do to get in trouble?
- Did you get into trouble very often?

What happened when you were caught?

- Sent to the principal
- Detention
- Suspended or expelled
- Punished by parents
- I was never caught!

#86 - TEACHERS

Did you have a favorite teacher, counselor, or coach?

- Why was this person special to you?

How did this teacher, counselor or coach influence you?

She Made All the Difference

by Ann Hamer

I really hated high school, and in my junior year I started skipping classes. At first just a few classes here and there, but eventually I'd skip for several days in a row. Back then, if you were absent you needed a note from home, so I became proficient at forging Mom's signature. I would show up for class every once in a while, and if it happened to be a test day, I would just sit and stare. I'd write my name at the top of the test paper and that would be it. It really threw my teachers for a loop. I remember one teacher saying that if I didn't take the test she'd have to flunk me. I told her to go ahead and flunk me. I just didn't care.

Mrs. Lillian Dean was my high school counselor. She kept me in school and made sure I graduated. Whenever I felt stressed or depressed, I would go talk with her. Sometimes I'd just hang out. She was responsible for over 400 students, but she always made time for me. Her office was my refuge. Mrs. Dean helped me graduate from high school in February, a semester early. I did not participate in the graduation ceremony in June, and did not see Mrs. Dean again after I graduated.

I hope I said thank you to Mrs. Dean back then, but I'm not sure I did. After all, I was a teenager. I wish I had contacted her later to say how much she meant to me. Maybe I didn't say it to her then, but I'm saying it now - thank you Mrs. Dean.

#87 - AFTER SCHOOL

What did you do after school?

- Musical instrument, singing, dance lessons
- Horseback riding lessons
- Soccer, football, track, gymnastics, swimming, other sports
- Boy or Girl Scouts
- Religious training
- Instruction in language and cultural traditions
- Online interactive gaming
- Hang out with friends
- Receive tutoring
- Neighborhood play with friends
- Care for younger siblings
- Housework and meal preparation
- Work in a family business or other part-time job
- Homework
- Or?

What activities did you start as a child that you later quit as you aged?

- Do you now regret your decision to quit?

Would you like to take up these activities again now that you are an adult?

- Will you?

#88 - SUMMERTIME

What did you do on a typical summer's day when you were not in school?

- As a child
- As a pre-teen
- As a teenager
- As a college/university student

Describe your activities

- Hang out with friends
- Work
- Babysit
- Read
- Go to summer school or work at an internship
- Play computer games
- Go to camp
- Play organized sports
- Travel
- Or?

#89 - CAMP

Did you go to camp?

- Day camp or sleep-away camp
- Scouting or church camp
- Special interest camp
- Leadership camp
- Music or drama camp
- Weight loss camp
- Outward Bound
- Science and math camp
- Sports camp
- Cheerleading or dance camp

Where was the camp?

- Did you go to camp more than once?

How old were you the first time you went to camp?

- Were you homesick?

What were your camp activities?

- Crafts
- Hiking
- Swimming and boating
- Horseback riding
- Campfire songs and skits
- Drama and music
- Winter sports
- Improving computer skills
- Improving leadership skills
- Science experiments
- Building and construction
- Gardening or farming
- Or?

Were you a camper, a counselor, or both?

#90 - SUMMER VACATION

Write about a summer memory from your childhood

- Where did you go?
- What did you do?
- Who was with you?
- What makes this memory so special?

Describe the things you always did with your family during the summer when you were a child

- Go to the beach
- Go to the family vacation home
- Go on family road trips
- Work in the family business

- Visit grandparents or other family members
- Or?

#91 - FINDING

Describe a time when you found something you weren't supposed to find or learned something you weren't supposed to know

- Family secret
- Business secret
- A hidden object
- Or?

How did it make you feel to learn this secret?

- Disappointed
- Relieved because it answered some of your questions
- Curious and made you want to know more
- Or?

#92 - PROCRASTINATE

Are you a procrastinator?

- What are you putting off until tomorrow that you should do today?

Will you eventually get around to doing these things?

HELPFUL HINT #13

CURING PROCRASTINATION

If you're anything like me, sometimes all the advice and all the Helpful Hints in the world just aren't enough. Sometimes you just don't want to do it. But no one else is going to do it for you, so you might as well get started and do it yourself!

Thanks to my experience as a world-class procrastinator, I have developed a few techniques to get myself moving. You may find them helpful.

- Try to make writing something you want to do, not something you have to do. If you find writing enjoyable, you will be less likely to procrastinate.

- When I am tempted to procrastinate, I tell myself I won't want to do it tomorrow any more than I want to do it right now, so I might as well do it today because then I won't lose sleep fretting, and I can congratulate myself for doing something I really did not want to do. For some reason this works for me.
- Break your project up into more manageable pieces by setting small tasks and deadlines for yourself.
- Start with the easiest part of your project. This will get you into the habit of writing and give you the satisfaction of completing a task.
- Do not let fear stop you. In writing your memoir it is almost impossible for you to make mistakes, because this is your story and how you tell your story is right for you. You only fail when you don't do it at all.
- Do not defeat yourself by being a perfectionist. Starting and moving forward should be your goal. You can make corrections and polish your writing during the editing process.
- If a way of doing a task stops working for you even if it "always" worked before, look for a new approach so you can move forward and achieve your goals.
- When you are tempted to give up, keep at your task for just five minutes more. When I give myself permission to stop after five minutes, I usually get involved with what I'm doing, and end up working for hours, not just minutes, more.
- You have an important story to tell, and the only one who can write your memoir is you. Get started by beginning with a basic prompt that makes it easy for you to write.

#93 - ACTING UP

Were you often in trouble as a child?

- How were you punished?

Who punished you?

- Parents or other family member
- Principal, teacher, coach
- Or?

Were these punishments fair?

What was the worst thing you did as a child?

- How were you punished?

#94 - CHILDHOOD DISAPPOINTMENT

Describe a disappointment from your childhood

- You didn't get the part
- You didn't get the A
- You didn't make the squad
- You didn't make the team
- You weren't asked to the dance
- You lost an election
- You realized there was no Santa
- You weren't allowed to do something you really wanted to do
- You weren't accepted by the popular kids
- You didn't have a best friend
- Or?

How did you deal with your disappointment?

- Cried
- Asked for an exception to the rule
- Sought help from a parent, teacher, or other adult
- Demanded a recount
- Complained to your friends
- Ran away from home
- Threw a tantrum
- Didn't let it bother you
- Or?

#95 - LESSONS FROM CHILDHOOD

What childhood moments or memories stand out in your mind as being especially important or influential?

- How did these events contribute to making you the adult you are today?

#96 - FAILURE

Describe a time when you failed

- Did you try again?
- If you did try again, did you succeed the second time?

If you did not try again, why not?

Remember success is not only achieving what you set out to do, it is also having the courage to re-examine your desires and expectations and set new goals for yourself. Sometimes failure is your heart's way of telling you to look elsewhere.

Bob vs. Alvin and the Macadamia Tree

by Peggy Nelson

When we purchased our house in Upland, we were thrilled and surprised to discover a full grown macadamia nut tree in our backyard. We never expected to see one grow in California, and especially not in OUR backyard. It soon became evident that our beautiful tree would also present a few problems. Not all was perfect in Nelsonville!!

In the summer the tree started producing, and soon became overloaded with the tiny immature little nuts. The tree then began casting them off on our patio! Another little cleanup chore for Bob, and a mess in our pool.

Alvin appeared in the middle of summer to start harvesting (and eating) OUR nuts! He became a wily little scavenger, and that really irritated Bob to no end. Out Bob went with the broom, acting like a crazed banshee, to scare Alvin off. Do you think that would faze that obstinate little squirrel? Not in the slightest. Alvin was so agile he could jump from the tree clear across the patio and even jump from up on the roof into the tree. He became very adept at dropping shells on a snoozing Bob lounging under the tree. So my infuriated husband decided to try:

First - A tack-on-the-tree repellant. Guaranteed to rid us of unwanted intruders. NO LUCK.

Second - A fake motion-sensor hooting owl. Maybe Alvin hooted more when he saw it. NO LUCK.

Third - A sonic-sensor device that was sure to do the trick. NO LUCK.

Fourth - Our son loaned Bob a BB gun, but that posed hazards for the neighbors if he missed the little critter ... soooo NO LUCK.

Alvin seemed bent on making amends. One day he tried to get into the house. He pounced twice on the glass at the patio door. We had other ideas. No squirrels allowed!!

Trying to live with both Bob and Alvin has become quite a feat. Solution: A truce. Live and let live. Little critters have to survive, and what would we do with so many, many nuts anyway? Share the wealth!

#97 - COLLEGE / UNIVERSITY

Did you go to college or university?

- What college or university did you attend?
- Why did you choose this one?

What was your major field of study?

- Why did you choose this major?
- Did you go to graduate school?

Did you win any awards or scholarships?

- Phi Beta Kappa or other academic honor societies
- Rhodes, Fulbright, or Marshall scholarships
- University honors program
- Academic, special interest, or sports scholarships

Did you compete for any awards or scholarships that you did not win?

- Why didn't you win?
- Did the winner deserve the award?
- How did you finance your education without the scholarship?

If you are currently in college, does rapid technological change ever make you feel that what you are learning will be obsolete by the time you graduate?

- How will your college education help you be competitive in the workforce or enable you to pursue your self-employment goals?

#98 - COLLEGE / UNIVERSITY HOUSING

Did you live at home or "go away" to school?

- How did you feel about leaving home for the first time?

If you did not live at home, where did you live?

- Dorm
- Fraternity or sorority house
- Off campus apartment or house
- Rented a room in someone's home

Did you have roommates?

- How did you choose your roommates?
- How did you get along?
- Did you become friends or not have much in common?
- Did you remain friends after you were no longer roommates?

#99 - COLLEGE / UNIVERSITY ACTIVITIES

Describe your extra-curricular activities

- Sorority/Fraternity
- Sports
- Clubs
- Internship or work-study program
- Volunteer activities
- Social or political activism
- Part time job
- And?

Describe your social life

- Parties
- Love
- Spring break vacations
- And?

#100 - STUDY ABROAD

Did you participate in a study abroad program?

- Where did you go and for how long?
- Were your classes in English or another language?
- Did you take advantage of travel opportunities while studying abroad?

Were you happy to return home or did you try to extend your time abroad?

#101 - COMMENCEMENT

Describe your degrees

- Bachelors degree
- Master's degree or doctorate
- Professional degrees, such as M.D. or J.D.
- Honorary degrees

If you did not complete your degree, why did you leave college?

- Did you later return and graduate?

Were you the first in your family to go to college or university or to earn a college degree?

- If you were not the first, who else in your family earned college or university degrees?
- Where did they attend college or university?

#102 - ANOTHER PATH

If you did not go to college or university, what did you do instead?

- Work
- Marry
- Have children
- Travel
- Learn a skilled trade
- Or?

If you chose not to go to college or university, did you later regret that decision?

- Do you plan to earn a college degree now that you are older?
- How would earning a college degree change your life?

#103 - TAKING THE TEST

What is the most difficult test you ever took?

- School
- Professional licensing, e.g. Bar exam, medical boards, nursing, or CPA exam
- Skilled trade licensing exam, e.g. electrician, beautician, plumber
- Citizenship exam
- Driving test

- Or?

How did you prepare?

Did you pass?

- If you failed the first time, how did you prepare to ensure you passed when you took it again?

What made it difficult for you?

- Subject matter was challenging
- The pressure to pass was too intense
- You didn't care enough to adequately prepare
- Or?

HELPFUL HINT #14

HELP OTHERS TELL THEIR STORY

If you are a caretaker or volunteer working with people who have difficulty writing or communicating, you can provide assistance, guidance, and encouragement to help them tell their stories. By using the tools in this book you can preserve their memories as a valuable legacy for family and friends.

See Appendix #1 for Guidelines for Caregivers

#104 - REUNION

Write the speech you'd like to give at your high school or college reunion

- What do you want your former classmates to know about you and your accomplishments?

How does the speech you would give at your 10th reunion differ from the speech you'd give at your 30th or 50th reunion?

#105 - WHO'S THAT?

Have you ever been on a blind date?

- How were you introduced?

How did it work out?

- Where did you go?
- What did you do?
- What did you talk about?
- Did you have anythng in common?

Did a romance or friendship develop, or was it just a one-time meeting?

#106 - ONLINE

Write your dating profile for Match.com

- Seeking a long-term relationship or just want to have some fun
- Your positive personality traits
- Your hobbies and interests
- A physical description of yourself
- What you must have in a partner
- What you absolutely will not accept in a partner

What attracts you to a person enough to want to pursue a relationship?

- Sense of humor
- Intelligence
- Certain physical characteristics
- Shared interests
- Common religious or political beliefs
- "Opposites attract"
- And?

Even if you do not want to post an online dating profile, this exercise helps you express in just a few words how you view yourself, your interests, and your values.

#107 - ROMANTIC LOVE

Have you ever loved or been loved by another person?

- By whom?

How did you meet?

- In class
- At work
- Chance meeting

- Blind date
- Set up by family or friends
- Online dating site or app such as Match.com or Tinder
- Or?

How did the relationship develop?

- Texting
- Dating
- Marriage
- Break-up, Divorce, Widowhood

Have you had more than one "true love"?

Love Ever After

by Sallie Ringle

Allen and I were married on May 8, 1966. Once we started dating we knew we were meant for each other, and married after six months. My parents were not in favor of the relationship because we were so young, but agreed to give us a small wedding in northern California.

The Vietnam War was going full storm and Allen did not have a deferment. The draft finally got him, and we were stationed in Germany for two years. Our son Don was born there. Once we returned to the US, Allen couldn't get work. We fought a lot. We were very frustrated and angry with life. My parents got involved and convinced me I needed to end my marriage. I was granted a divorce in 1970. I saw Allen a few times after that and at one point I thought we might be able to work things out. In the end I always got cold feet and was afraid of my parents' reaction. I married again for a second time in 1974.

Jump ahead to 2005. I was going to my son's wedding in San Diego. Both of my ex-husbands would be there. Talk about awkward. I hadn't seen Allen in 35 years. I really wanted to see him, talk to him, be in his presence. I decided I wouldn't be deterred by the awkwardness of the situation. "I know," I said to myself, "I'll ask our son Don." "Don, is Allen here?" "Yea" he replied. "Where?" I asked nonchalantly. I didn't want to give away that I was looking forward to our reunion. Don pointed Allen out to me.

When Allen turned around and I could see him fully, I really ogled. He was always the handsomest man I had ever known, and was still oh so handsome. Tall, 6'4", a shock of white hair that had thinned some, yet looked sexy on him. He was wearing a black suit with black T-shirt under the jacket. Very European looking. I kept watching him and waiting for the opportunity to make a move.

When he walked up to the bar, I sprang into action. "Hi Allen. It's good to see you after all this time. Don told me you were living in the Mariana Islands. Did you know I lived in Singapore for six years?" That was the beginning. I had spoken to the man I had never truly gotten over. The man I had always loved even though I was married to my second husband for 30 years. I loved Mike too. We had two daughters together and made a good life. But Allen had always been in my heart as my first and most true love. Our brief conversation sent butterflies and tingles through me. It was as though the years apart had never been. I felt almost giddy. Yet there was a sadness in me too. I had no idea what would happen after that Saturday in October 2005. Was that the end of us again? After all, he lived in Oregon, a little too far away to have a relationship.

About a month later I got a call from Allen. He said he thought maybe we should get together to talk. My heart started racing. Of course I wanted to meet with him. He was the love of my life. We made a plan that he would come to my house in Lake Arrowhead. I had no idea what would happen. After all, I had divorced him and taken his son away, and even had him give up parental rights so my second husband could adopt our son. I think I had good reason to be extremely anxious. I met Allen at the bottom of the mountain so he could follow me up to my house. I remember driving like a maniac. I wanted to be with him so much.

I made a special dinner. At first we were both tentative, not knowing what the other thought or felt. After dinner and a few glasses of wine we settled down comfortably. We shared our memories. I got out photos and said, "Remember this?" I brought out mementos I had saved from when we were together. The picture of the coast where we honeymooned. A sweater his mother had knit for me. Photographs of our son as a baby in Germany. At some point I giddily leaned over and kissed him on the cheek. Within minutes we were kissing and time stood still. We were passionate for each other. Allen spent that night with me, in fact he spent the next several days with me. Our son Don called Allen several times asking when he was coming to San Diego. All Allen said was, "When I decide to."

It has not been all perfect for us since then. I had a lot to learn about Allen's needs and how to meet them. I still had the bad habit of blurting out whatever came into my mind. I know I hurt his feelings often. But we were willing to work on our relationship and build a future together. At first we thought we would re-marry. I even made a wedding dress. As time passed we realized our relationship was good the way it was. We didn't need to marry.

Allen is devoted to me and I to him. I believe he cherishes me. I never grow tired of his loving touch and little squeezes. We laugh many times every day. He spoils me, doing all the cooking and lots of the cleaning. He understands me and puts up with my defects of character. He has inspired me to become who I am today. I know he has made me a better person over the last ten years. I don't know how many more years we have together, but I know that with Allen I am fulfilled. I am blessed to have found my soul mate again.

#108 - JOY

What gives you your greatest joy?

#109 - LOVE YOU

Write a love letter

#110 - CURRENT LOVE

Are you currently in a relationship?

- How long have you been together?
- Have you made a formal commitment to each other?

If you have not made a commitment, do you think your love will lead to a permanent relationship?

- Why or why not?
- When will you feel ready to make a commitment?

#111 - UNIQUE LOVE

What makes your love unique?

#112 - NOURISHING LOVE

How do you nourish your love?

- What can you do to continue nourishing your love?

How does love nourish you?

#113 - JEALOUS LOVE

When has your loved one done something to make you jealous?

- What did he/she do?

When have you made your loved one jealous?

- What did you do?

How was the issue resolved?

#114 - BREAKING UP

Describe a time when you broke up with someone or someone broke up with you

- What led to the break up?
- Was it a bad break up?

Did you try to get back together?

- If you did, how did it work out?

#115 - MARRIAGE (1)

Have you ever been married?

- Have you been married more than once?

Are you married now?

- Separated
- Divorced
- Widowed

How did you meet your spouse(s)?

- Describe your first encounter
- Describe your first date

Did you know your spouse was "the one" from the beginning, or did your love need time to grow?

- What did you like about this person?
- What did this person like about you?

Describe the proposal and engagement

- Where did the proposal take place?
- What was said?
- Was there a ring?
- Did your family support your choice?

If you had it to do all over again, would you still marry this person?

#116 - MARRIAGE (2)

If you never married (or remarried), why not?

- Never wanted to marry
- Never found the right person
- You were engaged, but did not get married
- Or?

#117 - WEDDING

Describe your wedding(s)

- Venue
- Guests
- Reception
- The things that went right
- The things that went wrong
- Most memorable wedding gift
- Your honeymoon(s)

If you have not yet had a wedding, how do you imagine it will be?

- Your spouse
- Your venue
- Your reception
- Your honeymoon

A Day at Dodger Stadium

by Jeanne Master

On the first Saturday in May it was Presbyterian Day at Dodger Stadium. Our church committed to a number of discounted tickets and a bus to take us there. My grandson Tyson had never seen a major league baseball game, so I decided to take him. I packed a lunch, took plenty of money, and off we went. The year was 1983.

We were enjoying the day and I was totally focused on my grandson when a man seated in front of us became very friendly. I was polite, but not interested in pursuing a friendship. The man kept turning around and talking to me. Later he told me he noticed I was not wearing a wedding ring, and was attracted to me. About the eighth inning he asked me what Presbyterian church I attended. The following Sunday I walked into church with two of my granddaughters. The man was there. He asked the usher my name and said, "She has a lot of kids." The usher, who knew me, answered, "Those are her grandchildren." For several Sundays this man found me on the patio after church to talk.

Finally he asked me out to dinner. I said, "No, but you can take me dancing." We went dancing at Industry Hills. Following that we took seven years of dancing lessons.

We fell in love and were married at our Presbyterian Church on December 26, 1983 with his four adult children and my three adult children in attendance, and my beloved brother Kenny giving me away. Two grandsons lit the candles at church and two granddaughters attended the guest book. A couple of hundred relatives and friends attended, and at the reception we danced and danced.

That Dodger Stadium flirt is still my husband, and we just celebrated our 30th wedding anniversary.

#118 - MARRIAGE HOME

Describe the first place you lived as a married couple

Describe the first home you bought as a married couple

#119 - NO LOVE

What if you hadn't fallen in love?

- "If I hadn't fallen in love, I would have ..."
- "I never fell in love because ..."

#120 - UNLOVED (1)

When did you realize that you weren't the love of his or her life?

- Do you still have feelings for this person?

#121 - UNLOVED (2)

Were you ever loved by someone you did not love?

- How did you tell this person you did not love him or her?

Were you able to be friends with this person?

#122 - LOST LOVE

Who or what is your lost love?

#123 - UNREQUITED LOVE

Do you have an unrequited love?

- Why were you and this person unable to get together?

Did you reconnect with this person after your feelings of attraction were over? If so, what happened?

- Your old feelings were rekindled
- You admitted to this person your former feelings
- There was no spark

Do you still have feelings for this person?

- Does this person now have any feelings for you?

4

HELPFUL HINT #15

MEMOIR VS. AUTOBIOGRAPHY

Memoir writing and autobiography are not the same thing. Autobiography is like Jack Webb in *Dragnet* - "Just the facts, Ma'am." Memoir records the stories of your life. It tells of the events that made you who you are and helps others get to know you better.

When memoirists write stories about love, grandparents, growing up, a favorite outfit or party, pets, career and challenges faced and lessons learned, not only do we get a sense of who they are as people, we also get a sense of their communities, their interests, and the people who surrounded them and formed the fabric of their lives. Recording when and where you were born, went to school, married, worked, resided, and traveled tells your readers just the facts. It is the special stories of your life that engage your readers and let them know who you truly are.

#124 - ARE YOU

Are you country or rock and roll?
A race car or a sedan?

A dog or a cat?

- Why?

#125 - IF YOU COULD

What would you do if you could?

- If money was no object
- If you had the necessary physical attributes
- If you had the required education and skills
- If you had the necessary innate talent

Here are some suggestions

- A job or career you would have
- A place you would travel
- A person you would love
- A sport you would play
- A thing you would create

#126 - FRUSTRATION

When are you frustrated?

- What causes your frustration?

#127 - SEASONS

What is your favorite season of the year?

- Why?

Is there a season you dread more than others?

- Why?

Do your memories impact how you feel about the seasons?

- Summer vacations and camp
- School starting in the fall
- Football games and homecoming
- Celebrating your birthday
- Traditional family get-togethers at certain times of the year

- Holiday celebrations
- Sports associated with certain seasons, e.g. ice skating in the winter and baseball in the spring
- Or?

#128 - WISE

Who is the wisest person you know

- What wisdom did this person share with you?

#129 - LONG

Think long thoughts.

- P.D. OUSPENSKY -

What are your long thoughts?

Writing Workshop: Day One
by Barbara Cauthorn

What is this? It's a big room and a small group of people. We're seated around three long tables, put together into a square. The chairs are comfortable, padded with an attractive red fabric. This is a writing workshop. What am I doing here? I drove over 1,000 miles for this? What is wrong with me? Everyone else is busy writing, thinking, concentrating, and creating interesting stuff. Look at the intensity on their faces. I have nothing to say.

The room is stuffy, without fans or air conditioning The shades are drawn to keep out the hot July sun. They are not accustomed to hot July sun here in northern Maine. There is a dream-catcher hanging on the wall over the fire extinguisher, next to the door marked EXIT. Is this a metaphor for something? Will all dreams be caught before you reach the exit sign?

I take another sip of cold coffee. I can't possibly do this. All my dreams must be stuck in that damned dream catcher.

I read this morning that you should just keep your hand moving during writing practice.

OK. My hand is moving and there are words on the paper. But they're meaningless garbage. There is no one at my side offering ideas; no ethereal guide appearing in an enlightened corner of my brain with clever words or good ideas. Nothing. Nada. Zilch. Empty.

When is lunch? Is it soon? I know how to eat lunch. I don't know how to do this.

#130 - SEX

Who first told you the truth about sex?

- Parents
- Siblings
- Friends
- Teachers or religious leaders
- Social media
- Or?

Where did you think babies came from before you learned the truth?

- What were your original ideas about sex?
- How old were you when you learned the truth?

How did you feel when you first learned the truth?

- Horror
- Curiosity
- Shock
- Amusement
- Disbelief
- Or?

#131 - CONSCIENCE

How does your conscience guide you?

- How are you an honorable person?

When does your conscience bother you?

- In what ways are you dishonorable?

#132 - PERMISSION

Describe a situation in which you acted without first obtaining permission

- Did you later need to ask for forgiveness?

What were the results of your action?

#133 - COMMUNICATIONS

Describe the most exciting telephone call, letter, or email you ever received

- Job offer
- College acceptance
- Love letter
- Renewed contact from a long-lost relative or friend
- Unexpected money
- Announcement of an engagement
- Announcement of a pregnancy or birth
- Something you won
- Or?

Were you ever deceived by an exciting message that turned out to be false or a scam?

- Were you able to protect yourself before you lost any money or had your identity stolen?
- If you were the victim of identity theft, what happened and how did you deal with it?

#134 - KNOWING

What do you know to be true about yourself?

- "I am …"
- "I value …"
- "I love …"
- And?

HELPFUL HINT #16

GATHER TOGETHER

Gather together with family and friends to look at old photos, talk and share memories. Ask about their memories of you; after all, this is your story. But remember, you don't live in a vacuum, so ask them for their memories of their own lives. Their lives have touched yours and are part of your story.

#135 - PHOTOS

Go through your photos and select a picture of yourself

- Why did you select this photo?
- What about this photo appeals to you?
- When and where was this photo taken?
- Who is in this photo with you?
- What story does this photo tell?

How do you look in this photo?

- Were you surprised by the way you look when you first saw this photo?
- Do you look different in this photo than you thought you looked when it was taken?
- Do you look better? Worse?

#136 - HAPPY AND GOOD

Go do something that makes you feel happy and write about it

Go do something that makes you feel good and write about it

#137 - COMPLIMENTS

What is the best compliment you ever received?

- Did the compliment surprise you?

What is the best compliment you ever gave?

- How was your compliment received?

#138 - DREAMS

Write about a time when your dreams came true

#139 - PUTTERING

What do you do when you putter?

#140 - INFLUENCE

What person had the greatest influence on you when you were growing up?

- What did this person say or do that was so influential?

Was this person a continuing influence, or was their influence the result of a single action or incident?

How did this person's influence impact you?

- Was the influence positive or negative?

Does this person's influence continue to impact you?

My Granddad
by Aurora Reinhart

My mom's father was my Granddad Eliseo Hernandez. I loved him dearly. Today, as days go by I feel that his image in my mind is slowly fading away. I am afraid I will lose his handsome debonair image. It's sad there were no pictures taken of him. Life was difficult then, and picture taking was the last thing they would spend money on. I am thankful I have this chance to try to recreate his image, his beautiful home and garden, his simple and contented life. According to my parents he was soooo happy when I was born. I was his first granddaughter and the first to survive. My first two brothers had died in infancy. I loved spending my summer vacations with him. As soon as school closed for summer, he took a bus to our house in Manila, spent a few days for a visit, and then took me back with him to the province where he lived.

His house was located in the Pampanga region of the Philippines in a small barrio called San Antonio. The house had a nipa roof, varnished bamboo beams, wooden walls, varnished bamboo flooring, and large windows. The house was huge and the rooms airy. The Philippines has a tropical climate, hot and humid. His house was well ventilated and comfortable. I loved walking barefoot on the smooth shiny floors that were kept clean and shiny by being polished with dry banana leaves. We ate in a corner by the dining room and sat on the floor. The dining table had twelve inch legs like Japanese tables. We ate with our clean washed hands. I enjoyed those meals. He always had a story to tell as we ate.

There were no ovens or electric stoves. Cooking was a big task. People had to collect wood and build kindling before the fire could start. I saw my aunt and step-grandmom blowing and fanning before the kindling got started. My granddad built a two burner concrete stove. I called it The Beast. It had a funnel for rice husk fuel. He got the rice husks from a nearby mill. The ashes from the burned rice husks were funneled down through a pipe that went through the flooring to the ground. The ashes were used to clean pots and pans. "Comet Cleanser" in today's world.

My grandfather passed away when I was 16 years old. I was beyond myself. I missed him dearly, and miss him even now. I am truly glad I will remember him again every time I read this short story I wrote about him.

#141 - THE FIRST TIME

Write about the first time you

- Kissed someone in a romantic way
- Had a "crush"
- Drove a car
- Bought a car
- Rented an apartment
- Lived by yourself
- Traveled away from home
- Traveled to a foreign country
- Earned a paycheck
- Fell in love
- Had sex
- Gave a speech
- Rode a bike
- Went on a diet

- Made a best friend
- Snuck out of the house
- Flew in an airplane
- Took a real vacation
- Shot a gun
- Won a prize
- Earned an "A"
- Flunked a class
- Forgot your lines
- Went to a concert
- Ate at a "fancy" restaurant
- Voted in an election
- Taught a new skill
- Learned a new skill
- Wore formal clothing
- Drank too much
- Stole something
- Opened a bank account
- Got a credit card

#142 - HERO WORSHIP

Who is your hero?

- What is it about this person that you admire?

Is there a person you once worshipped, but now no longer admire?

- What caused this person to fall from favor in your eyes?

#143 - FAMOUS PEOPLE

Describe your encounters with famous people

#144 - TALENT

What are your talents?

- What things do you have absolutely NO talent for?

What talents do you wish you had?

#145 - WISHING (1)

What do you wish you could do?

- Play an instrument, dance, sing
- Write a bestseller
- Win an Oscar, Nobel Prize, Olympic medal
- Climb Mount Everest
- Bike across the country
- Hike the Appalachian Trail
- Play in a championship athletic contest
- Star in a movie or Broadway show
- Meet a famous person
- Be a famous person
- Give a speech
- Invent something
- Travel in space
- Or?

What can you do to fulfill your wishes?

#146 - WISHING (2)

What do you wish was true?

HELPFUL HINT #17

DATE WHAT YOU WRITE

Not only do you want to accurately date the events from your past, you also want to note the date on which you write down your stories. Your life changes as time passes, and by dating what you write you will know how you felt during different stages of your life.

#147 - AMBITION

Are you an ambitious person?

What was your ambition

- As a child
- As a young adult
- In mid-career
- As a senior
- Now

Did you achieve your ambitions?

How did your ambitions change as you aged?

- Do you still have ambitions you hope to achieve?

#148 - WORK AND CAREER

Describe your working life

- Paid and unpaid jobs
- Homemaker or work outside the home
- First job
- Part-time jobs
- Summer jobs
- Internships

Describe your career path

- Jobs you loved
- Jobs you hated
- Jobs you applied for and did not get
- Jobs you quit
- Jobs you lost – fired or laid off

How were you able to use your special skills and talents on the job?

- What were you really good at on the job?

What was the favorite of your jobs?

- What was the job that "got away"?

Was there a job you did not take (either refused an offer or no offer was made) that had you taken it, may have changed your career path?

- How would it have changed your career path?

#149 - YOUR EMPLOYERS

Describe your employers

- The best company you ever worked for? Why?
- The worst company you ever worked for? Why?
- Your best boss or supervisor? Why?
- Your worst boss or supervisor? Why?

#150 - MENTORING

Were you ever mentored?

- Who mentored you?
- What did this person do to mentor you?

Did you ever mentor another person?

- Who?
- What did you do to help this person?
- How did having you as a mentor impact this person's career?

How did having or not having a mentor impact your career path?

#151 - WORK AND CAREER ACCOMPLISHMENTS

What makes you most proud when you think about your working life?

- Accomplishments
- Promotions and raises
- Innovations you created
- Triumph over difficult situations
- Friendships
- And?

What regrets do you have about your working life?

#152 - LOSS OF EMPLOYMENT

Have you ever been fired from a job?

- What reasons were you given for being fired?
- In your opinion, what was the *real* reason you were fired?

Was the firing expected or unexpected?

What did you do after you were fired?

- Promptly found another job
- Collected unemployment
- Filed a grievance or lawsuit
- Got depressed and went into hiding
- Moved because you could no longer afford your home or needed a fresh start
- Or?

In retrospect, do you think the firing was justified?

#153 - SIMPLE

If you can't explain something simply, you don't really understand it.

- BILL GATES -

Explain simply something that you know how to do very well

#154 - GOALS

Describe a goal you set for yourself and achieved

Do you have goals you have not yet achieved?

- Will you continue trying to achieve these goals?

#155 - ADVERSITY

What did you accomplish in the face of adversity?

#156 - THE AX

As a supervisor, have you ever fired another person?

- What did you say to this person?

How did firing this person make you feel?

- Worried about this person's future, even though it had to be done
- Glad to see the person go
- Ambivalent - it was just part of your job

Were there any unpleasant repercussions as a result?

- Lawsuits
- Threats
- Complaints filed with government agencies or your employer
- Or?

#157 - RUN AWAY (2)

Have you ever run away now that you are an adult?

- Why did you run away?
- Where did you go?
- How were you treated when you returned home?

Have you run away more than once?

- If you haven't yet run away, do you think you ever will?

HELPFUL HINT #18

GET A COLORING BOOK

Coloring can be relaxing, free up your mind, and keep you from obsessing about difficulties you may have with your writing. There are many places to purchase coloring books with sophisticated designs that are relaxing and fun to color. When I was a kid, there was nothing better than being the proud owner of the giant orange box of 64 Crayola crayons. So get yourself a coloring book and some crayons or colored pencils, and get started. Let your mind wander as you color. Be sure to keep a pen and paper handy to jot down the thoughts that occur to you as you color.

My friend Susan suggested that you use the pages you color as chapter dividers in your memoir. What a great idea!

#158 - DREAM JOB

The only way to do great work is to love what you do.

- STEVE JOBS -

Describe your dream job or career

- Describe the job you always believed you'd be great doing

Did you actually get this dream job or have this dream career?

- Did the reality of having this job live up to your expectations?

If you never had your dream job, why not?

- Too costly to pursue the required education
- Feelings of insecurity and doubt
- Time issues
- Family issues
- Physical fitness or physical ability limitations
- You did what was "right" or "sensible" rather than pursue your dream job
- You were expected to go into the family business
- You tried but it just never worked out for you
- You didn't have the necessary talents or abilities
- Other commitments
- Or?

#159 - BEST JOB

Who do you believe has the best job in the world?

- Why?

Would you like to do this job?

- Will you ever have the chance?

#160 - CARPE DIEM

How do you seize the day?

#161 - ALONE

Describe a time when you were lonely

- Lonely as a child
- Lonely as a teen
- Lonely as an adult
- Lonely by yourself
- Lonely in a crowd
- Lonely now

I am never lonely because

- I can always find ways to amuse myself
- I value my privacy and need my alone time
- Or?

#162 - BECAUSE

In one of my autobiography classes we wrote about favorite outfits. Jeanne wrote about a black dress and matching hat she bought, "Because I could."

After class I thought a lot about that phrase - "Because I could". It tells so much and could describe so many things: triumph over difficulties, adventures you had, things you bought or vacations you took, surviving an illness, changes in status, or something you did against all odds.

Write about something you did "because you could"

What does this phrase mean to you?

- Freedom to make choices
- Coming through a difficulty, challenging time, or illness
- Change in monetary, residence, or relationship status allowing you to do something, buy something, or go somewhere that was not previously possible
- Finding a source of inner courage or strength
- A chance to have an adventure
- A feeling of independence upon reaching adulthood
- Feeling a new sense of maturity
- A chance to rebel
- Or?

How did it make you feel to do something because you could?

The Simple Black Dress

by Jeanne Behr

The year was 1955 in Denver, Colorado. I had just graduated from high school and found a job at the Mountain States Telephone Company in downtown Denver. It was a fun job working with women my own age.

During my lunch hour or after work, I would shop at the big name department stores nearby. One day I found a simple black dress and hat. I could wear them on dates and to church. Being young and single, I bought them because I could! As life moved on after marriage and children, moments of "Because I could" were few and far between, if ever again!

By the way - I still have the dress.

#163 - CLOTHES

What is (or was) your favorite outfit?

- Why is it so special?

Describe an occasion when you wore this outfit

- How did it make you feel?

What happened to this outfit?

- Gave it to someone else
- Donated it
- Sold it at a garage sale or on consignment
- You still have it
- You still have it and still wear it

#164 - TRADITIONAL CLOTHING

Describe a time when you wore a garment traditional to your cultural, ethnic, or religious heritage that you do not usually wear

- Kippah or hijab

- Lederhosen, kilt, kimono, hanbok, serape, sari, etc.
- Kufi or gele
- Or?

How did you feel the first time you wore this garment?

- Proud
- Embarrassed or self-conscious
- Connected to your ancestors
- Or?

When do you currently wear this garment?

#165 - CHARM

The third time's a charm

HELPFUL HINT #19

YOUR OWN UNIQUE SELF

You are a compelling person with a unique point-of-view. Your speaking voice, your actions, your physical appearance, and your hopes and dreams are all unique to you. When you write the story of the compelling and unique person your family and friends love, they will want to keep reading and get to know you better.

When you are true to yourself, you establish an emotional connection to the people for whom you are writing your memoir. Don't disguise yourself. You're not perfect; no one is. Include all of your lumps, bumps, and warts. When you do that, your readers will trust your honesty, and recognize and treasure you as the person they love. They will keep reading in order to share your experiences and your life.

#166 - ATTITUDE

Are you an

- Optimist
- Pessimist
- Realist

- Pragmatist

Why?

#167 - NEED

What is it you really need?

- As a child
- As a teen
- As a young adult
- In middle age
- Now

Did you ever get it?

#168 - CURIOSITY

What made you curious when you were a child?

- Are you still curious about these things?

What makes you curious now?

#169 - MEANINGFUL

What makes your life meaningful?

#170 - DRIVING

How, when, and where did you first learn to drive a car?

- Who taught you?

Describe your first car

- Did your first car have a name?

Have you received any traffic tickets?

- What did you do to receive the tickets?
- How were you treated by the officer who ticketed you?
- Did you fight the ticket?

Has your license ever been revoked?

- What caused you to lose your license?
- For how long was your license revoked?
- Did you have to do anything special to regain your license, e.g. take a class, get treatment for substance abuse, etc.

If you never learned to drive, what was the reason for your decision?

- How do you get around since you don't drive a car?

#171 - CAR ACCIDENTS

Describe any car accidents you've had

- Caused by you
- Caused by others

Have you seriously injured someone or been seriously injured while driving a car?

- Describe the accident
- What were the long term impacts of these serious injuries?

#172 - ROAD TRIP

Describe the first road trip you took in which you were the driver

- What car were you driving?
- Did you go by yourself or with others?
- How many miles did you travel?
- How long were you away from home?

Where did you go?

- Why did you choose this destination?

How did you feel as you drove away from home?

- Excited
- Nervous
- Scared
- Eager
- Happy
- Lighthearted

- Adventurous
- Daring
- Grown-up
- Or?

#173 - CHILDHOOD LEGACY

The first eighteen years of your life were filled with the intensity of many firsts: first steps, first words, first friends, first love, first disappointment, first loss, first success. During your teens, your emotions and hormones swept you from joy to despair, often in a matter of minutes. The adult you grew into and the adult you are today is the direct descendant of the child and the teenager that you once were.

What do you want your future readers to know about your childhood and the person you were as both a child and a teen?

- What were some of the defining moments or important people from your childhood?
- What childhood memories are closest to your heart?

5

HELPFUL HINT #20

THINK ABOUT YOUR FUTURE

You may think that you are not old enough to write your memoirs. You have not yet completed college, started your career, married or had children, and you are still decades away from retirement.

Let me assure you that this book is for people of all ages, including the young. My friend Madison, who is still a university student, said that what she likes about the writing prompts, even when they do not apply to her present life, is that they give her a chance to think about her vision for her life and her hopes for the future.

Use the writing prompts to help you think about your own future. How do you envision your career? Do you see yourself marrying or having children? Where do you want to travel and make your home? Write down the thoughts, hopes, and dreams you have for both your present and your future life, and when you reread these writings years from now, you will be amazed by the great wisdom you possessed when you were young.

#174 - BECAUSE OF YOU

The world is before you, and you need not take it or leave it as when you came in.

- JAMES BALDWIN -

What exists because you are here?

#175 - PAST

Think about who you were at age 25, and give that person some advice

- What do you want the younger you to know?

If the person you were at age 25 had followed this advice, what difference would it have made?

- To your life?
- To your studies and choice of college or university?
- To your career?
- To your relationships?
- To your friendships?
- To your finances?
- To where you now live?

#176 - FUTURE

If you are not yet 25, imagine yourself at that age and give that person some advice based on your present experience and knowledge

#177 - DEAR DIARY

Write a diary entry or letter to yourself dated ten years from now

- What will your life be like in ten years?

Where will you be living?

- Your first apartment or house
- Where you live now

- In your family home
- Moved to a larger home
- Moved to a more suburban or rural home
- Downsized and moved to a smaller home
- Mobile home
- In a senior community
- Camper, tent, recreational vehicle
- Moved in with a child or friend
- No fixed address

What will you be doing?

- Going to school
- Working
- Starting a second career
- Retired
- Volunteer work
- Traveling
- Spending time with family and friends
- Learning a new sport or skill
- Writing a book
- Or?

How will you look?

- Describe the state of your health and well-being

Sum up your previous ten years of life

- Things you want to do
- Places you want to visit
- Relationships you want to have
- Accomplishments
- And?

#178 - HOW DO YOU LOOK?

Describe the way you look

- Hair and eye color
- Height

- Body type
- Your best physical feature

Were you ever told that you looked like someone else?

- Your mother or father
- A sibling or other family member
- A famous person

What do you like about your physical appearance?

- Is there something about your physical appearance you now like that you once disliked?

If you could change one thing about your physical appearance, what would it be?

- What about your physical appearance makes you feel insecure?

#179 - MUSICAL

What musical instrument do you play?

- How long have you been playing this instrument?
- Why did you choose to study this instrument?

Did you sing in a school, church, or community choir?

- Did you perform in musicals in your school or community theater?

Have you ever been a solo artist?

- Describe a memorable solo performance

Do you still play the instrument or sing?

- If not, why did you quit?

#180 - CONCERT

Write about the first concert you attended

- Name of the performer(s)
- Venue
- Music genre - classical, rock, folk, gospel, hip hop, country, alternative, etc.

Who went with you?

What aspects of the performance do you remember?

- A particular song

- Light show or dance
- The crowd
- Or?

Did you have a personal encounter with the performer(s) after the concert?

HELPFUL HINT #21

BE ENTHUSIASTIC

As you read the memoirs and autobiographies of others, notice the difference between a story that engages you and a story that leaves you flat. I think the difference is enthusiasm. Don't stand apart from your life when you're telling your story. If you tell your story with energy and enthusiasm, it will come alive for your readers.

Be interested in what you write. If you don't care about your story, don't expect others to care. If you don't find yourself and your life interesting, your readers certainly won't find you interesting either.

#181 - ROOMIES

With whom, besides a spouse or significant other, have you shared a room, apartment, or house?

- College roommate(s)
- Sharing with friends
- Renting a room in someone's house
- Sharing with a sibling or other relative
- Sharing with a traveling companion
- Staying with the parents or family of a friend

How did you get along with your roommate(s)?

- Was there anything about your roommate(s) that drove you crazy?
- Did you drive your roommate(s) crazy?

Are you still friends?

#182 - CITY

What is your favorite city?

- What is it about this city that you love?

Do you live in or make regular visits to this city?

- If you don't live in this city, would you like to?
- Do you have any plans to move to this city?

#183 - COUNTRY

What is your favorite country?

- What is it about this country that you love?

Do you live in or make regular visits to this country?

- If you don't live in this country, would you like to?
- Do you have any plans to move to this country?

#184 - QUOTE

What is your favorite quote?

- Why is it your favorite?

#185 - CHANCE (1)

Describe a chance meeting that changed everything

- What was changed?

#186 - CHANCE (2)

Describe a random conversation that changed everything

- With whom were you talking?
- What was the topic of the conversation?
- What was changed?

#187 - IS A HOUSE A HOME

Where is truly home to you?

What makes it home?

- The people who live there
- The location
- The house itself

Has your concept of "home" changed as you've aged?

Where is the place you feel was most truly home?

- Where you live now
- A residence where you once actually lived
- A place you saw while traveling
- A place you saw on television or the internet
- A place you've read or heard about
- The home where you grew up
- The home where you raised your family
- You have never lived in a place you felt was truly home

If you no longer live in this home, what happened to cause you to leave?

- A required move to another city
- Divorce or other changes to the family unit
- Change in financial status
- You grew up and became an adult
- Wanderlust
- Or?

Earthquakes

by Joan Wallach

with gratitude to Cindy Reed

We were in our honeymoon phase ... a friendship had blossomed into love. Arthur, the New Yorker, had a Denver decade under his belt and was happily reacquainting me with my hometown after 15 years away. Denver - still a cow town, land locked, high, and dry. Denver - 300 days of sunshine, surrounding mountains' majesty, family and friends. Home.

We went to see Joan Baez at a venue now gone. We were transported by the music, brought back to the best in each other as we exited into the crisp autumn night. The next morning began with a shattering - though not unexpected - phone call. It was Arthur's brother Alan calling from San Francisco. Alan couldn't get out of bed. He needed an ambulance and needed Arthur to tell their parents why. Arthur knew Alan was living with AIDS, but Alan hadn't told anyone else. He had never come out to his parents. In crisis it was both easy to forgive a brother's cruel omissions and hell to make the unthinkable call.

We spoke of moving to San Francisco. We'd be there for Arthur's parents and could spend Alan's remaining time with him. San Francisco, a cultural and food mecca, was certainly alluring. Living together seemed a good step. Arthur's daughters would be close to their grandparents. We packed. We looked for a home. We researched schools. Arthur commuted every two weeks.

We visited that Halloween. It was ghoulish. Arthur's mother was disoriented and disconnected, her lung cancer having metastasized to her brain. And all too fast, Alan was declining. What could I do? I made applesauce, filling his home with the smells of cloves and cinnamon, but Alan declined the Cranes stationery with its eighth inch green trim. Weak, but with sensibilities intact, he proclaimed, "It's a little much."

Next trip - the surreal holiday visit. Christmas lights without snow and leaves still on the trees. Arthur and I shuttling from one hospital ward to another. Arthur's mother dying in one building, Alan struggling in the other. Rose died at the end of November. As we approached the synagogue, Alan fell. His weakness spoke to us in ways his mother's impersonal and sparsely attended funeral could not. Five weeks later, after morphine infused talk of a Mobius strip, Alan died. For his funeral we called in Denver family, and stayed up late into the night, weaving memories into a eulogy befitting this absent 48 year old man.

Finally, our move was complete. We settled in a rental home in the Berkeley Hills. We became a cobbled together family, with all its drama and angst. I was 33, the littlest of fish in the giant pond of San Francisco.

And yet. There were amazing inexpensive Chinese dinners, and long walks on Solano Avenue. There were bookstores aplenty, flowers in winter, wins for both daughters as they found their new people. There were stunning concerts, readings, sunsets at the ocean, morning buns and seedy baguettes ...

And yet again. There was the business. Theft, suicide, and vast debt preceded us. I lived to tell the tale of the burned out tax auditor who, on the cusp of retirement, looked at my boxes of documents, said something about my honest face, and gave us a reprieve.

What finally punctured our hope and resolve? Was it alarm company calls alerting us to business break-ins at 2:00 and 3:00 a.m.? Was it the collection calls from suppliers which penetrated Arthur's dreams and served as waking nightmares? Could it have been the 7.9 Richter scale earthquake that shook each of us to our core?

We stayed as long as we could. After the girls graduated from high school. After we married, exchanging rings symbolic of the Mobius strip. After the Oakland A's lifted us up. After Arthur's dad found a new companion. Only then could Arthur say what haunted him. He was lonely and overwhelmed. His losses compounded every day. He wanted out. It had taken seven years and aftershocks from losing Alan and Rose too numerous to count.

It was time to go home.

#188 - REFUGE

Where do you take refuge?

- When do you feel the need for refuge?

#189 - DISASTER

Just because you've lost everything material doesn't mean you've lost everything.

- AMERICAN RED CROSS PUBLIC SERVICE ANNOUNCEMENT -

In 2017, the world saw huge destruction and loss due to hurricanes, floods, and fires. When all is lost and you return home to nothing, what you still have are your memories. Sometimes that is all you have. Remembering is a way to rebuild and a way to heal. Memoir writing is not just about where you were born, went to school, worked, and the person you married. It is also about release, forgiveness, catharsis, and ultimately hope and healing.

Write about a natural disaster that changed your life

- Tornado
- Earthquake
- Fire
- Flood
- Drought
- Storm
- Monsoon, tropical storm, hurricane
- Lightening strike

What happened?

- Loss of life
- Loss of residence
- Loss of other property
- Loss of lifestyle
- Loss of livelihood
- Or?

What did you do to recover?

#190 - HUNGER

What are you hungry for right now?

#191 - DOING RIGHT

Write about a time when you did the right thing

#192 - WRONG

Describe a time when you were wrong

#193 - VANITY

What have you done to satisfy your vanity?

- Plastic surgery
- Spa treatments

- Crash diets
- Participating in sports or activities generally done by younger or more athletic people
- Or?

How did it make you feel to do these things?

- Glad - I feel better because I look better
- I wasted my time and money
- Younger
- Or?

HELPFUL HINT #22

KEEP 'EM GUESSING

It is important that you capture your readers with your first few sentences. You are not writing a school essay, so stay away from formal introductions that slow the pace of your narrative. You want to engage your readers by telling your story, not explaining it. Let your readers share the experience of being you.

You want your readers to keep reading, so don't give away your story in the first few paragraphs. Hold some things back and don't strip yourself bare in the early pages. Use an unexpected word or phrase to leave your readers guessing so they want to come back for more.

#194 - DIVINE

The ancient Hindu expression Namaste means "The divine in me honors the divine in you."

What is the divine in you?

- What divine do you see in others?

How do you honor the divine?

#195 - CINQUAIN

A cinquain is a five-line poem. The first line of the poem has one word, the second line two words, the third line three words, the fourth line four words, and the fifth line one word.

For example:

Cookies
gulped down
can give me
an extra added pound
tomorrow

They can be simple and fun or meaningful and elegant. You choose.

Write a cinquain

#196 - GADGET

Write about a gadget or invention that makes your life easier

- Credit cards and online banking
- Computers
- Post-it notes
- Staples and paper clips
- Refrigerator, stove, washer and dryer, microwave, dishwasher
- Cars, bikes, Segway, hoverboard
- Airplanes
- Electricity and light blubs
- Telephones, smart phones, tablets, iPads
- Apps
- Wifi and the internet
- Energy drinks
- Indoor plumbing
- Modern medical equipment
- Air conditioning
- Television and Netflix
- And?

How old were you when you first used this invention?

- How did this invention change your life?

Do you have an idea for an invention that makes life easier?

#197 - YOUR SENSES

Describe your favorite (or least favorite) smell, sight, touch, taste, or sound

- Why it is your favorite (or least favorite)?

When you experience this sense, what is your reaction?

- What does it make you do?
- How does it make you feel?
- What does it mean to you?
- What memories does it awaken?
- In what parts of your body do you sense it?

How have your senses changed as you've aged?

- Is there a sense you never had, lost, or no longer have full use of?
- How does not having this sense impact you?

Are you more or less sensitive to certain things - noises too loud, lights too dim, print too small where it was once large enough - than you used to be?

- How does this sensitivity impact you?

Redondo

by Ann Hamer

The Helms Bakery truck. The distinctive sound of its whistle - whoo, whoo. The delicious-ness when the drawer of donuts was pulled open and out wafted that sweet yeasty sugary golden smell. Even after all these years I can still see the driver swing open the rear doors of his truck and pull out that polished wooden drawer full of donuts. And I still smell it - that perfect fat shiny glazed donut. Anyone who grew up in Southern California at that certain time knows exactly what I mean.

My brothers and I weren't allowed to buy donuts from the Helms man. Mom always said that if we were hungry after school we could have a piece of fruit. But Nancy, who lived at the bottom of the hill, bought a donut every day - probably because she was so skinny. Nancy's mother had a VW van, and Nancy, Lynda, Judy, and I would sit in the van when it was parked in Nancy's driveway and pretend to be the Beatles on tour. I was Ringo, Nancy was George, Lynda was John, and Judy was Paul.

Playing with Judy was always the best fun because she had such an incredible imagination. Our Barbies had the most amazing adventures. Sometimes they were at a Swiss boarding school, and sometimes they owned a horse ranch, and sometimes they were spies, intriguing with James Bond and Jim Phelps. We may have been at Judy's house playing Monopoly, but in our minds we were riding the Orient Express, negotiating with the mysterious strangers who shared our compartment. I can still feel the excitement of the stories Judy wove around that simple game of Monopoly we played in her living room one rainy Redondo night.

#198 - CRAZY

Did you ever have a crazy money making scheme?

- What was it?

Did you try to implement your scheme?

- What happened?

#199 - SHORTFALL

One time when I was desperate for cash, I ...

- Called my parents
- Begged
- Sold my blood
- Pawned my possessions
- Turned a trick
- Borrowed from the wrong person
- Did someone else's work for them
- Wrote a paper or took a test for another person
- Or?

What happened to make you so short of cash?

- How did you get back on your feet?

#200 - PERFECT

Describe your most perfect day

- Perfect holiday
- Perfect place visited
- Perfect day of school
- Perfect day with family
- Perfect celebration
- Wedding
- Birth of a child
- Graduation
- Significant milestone
- Perfect day being with another person or group of people
- Or?

#201 - HAVING A GOOD TIME

What is the best time you ever had?

- Where were you?
- What happened that was so enjoyable?
- Who was with you?

What memory still makes you smile when you think about it?

#202 - FICTIONAL

What fictional or cartoon character would you like to be?

- What about this character attracts you?

How are you like this character in real life?

- How are you unlike this character?

HELPFUL HINT #23

MAKING LISTS

Making lists can help jog your memory. Your lists may bring to mind people and things you have not thought about for many years.

Here are some suggestions for lists to work on

- Family and friends
- Schools attended and degrees earned
- Residences
- Books read
- Movies seen
- Places visited
- Concerts, plays, or sporting events attended
- Classes taken
- Toys and games played
- Pets and animals you've known

Don't spend too much time preparing to write by making endless lists. It's easy to convince yourself that you're being productive when you're really just doing busy work. Keep your objectives in mind and use your lists to get you started and keep you writing!

#203 - JEWELRY

Do you have a special or favorite piece of jewelry?

What is its significance?

- Wedding or engagement ring
- Class ring
- First piece of "real" jewelry you owned
- Family heirloom
- A piece of jewelry that belonged to a parent or grandparent
- Gift from a special person
- Memento of a special event

- Something special you bought for yourself

When do you wear this piece of jewelry?

- Everyday
- On special occasions
- Never - It's too valuable, too old-fashioned, or kept in a safety deposit box

Who will receive this piece of jewelry when you no longer want it or need it?

- Who will inherit your jewelry?
- Why did you choose this person as the recipient?

#204 - AGAIN

Describe your recurring dreams

#205 - POLITE

How are you polite?

- When are you polite?

Was there a time when being rude was your only option?

- Why?

What happened as a result of your rudeness?

#206 - PARENTAL GUIDANCE (1)

What are the concepts and values you learned as a child that you taught to your own children or grandchildren?

#207 - PARENTAL GUIDANCE (2)

Did you raise your children in any particular religious tradition?

- Attendance at services and classes
- Prayer
- Religious based camps and summer school

How important to your family was practicing your religion?

- Very, we attended services and actively participated at least once a week
- Not very, our participation was usually limited to holidays or special occasions like weddings, baptisms, first communion, and bar/bat mitzvah

Do your children and grandchildren still practice this religious tradition?

#208 - BABIES

Are you a "baby" person?

- How did you feel the first time you held a baby?

What baby has meant the most to you?

- First child
- First grandchild
- First daughter
- First son
- Younger sibling
- Someone else's baby who made you think you might want your own child
- A puppy or kitten

Did you babysit when you were a child or teenager?

- Was caring for babies something you enjoyed or an unwanted obligation?

The First Time I Held A Baby

by Susan Fraizer

The first baby I remember holding was my sister Carol. She was so small. She only weighed four pounds and a few ounces when she was born. She was fussed over quite a bit by my grandfather and me. I thought she was the cutest baby ever. She had white blond hair and the biggest blue eyes. Her hair was so fuzzy and white that you had to look really hard to see it. My grandfather would let me hold her when I sat on the couch in the living room. She hardly moved and her cries were so soft. She had a hard time as she coughed a lot. She made it though, and I am so thankful for that. My mother would put her bassinet deep in the closet. It really bothered me that she was way back in the dark. I sneaked in there all the time to check on her. I adored being her big sister.

I found my sister Carol to be such a joy in my life. I watched over her and loved every moment of it. My two other sisters were not thrilled with her and were mean to her. She was not as strong as the rest of us. When she was old enough to ride a tricycle she could not keep up with the three of us on our bicycles. The other two called her names and I would chase them away. She would still try to keep up on her tricycle. I would get off my bicycle and hold on to the handle bars of the trike with her and scoot my foot on the pavement to help her go faster. She would squeal with delight at being able to keep up. That is what it is like to this day. Always standing together.

We are best friends and there is nothing that could ever come between us. I feel God blessed me in giving me such a beautiful sister.

#209 - PARENTING

Do you have children?

- Biological and adopted children
- Stepchildren
- Foster children

What are the names of your children?

- Why were they given these names?
- What are their nicknames?

Write something about each of your children

- Their physical appearance
- Their character
- Their accomplishments
- What makes you proud
- A favorite toy or activity of each child
- A memory of each child that makes you smile

Which parent does each child take after?

- How are each of your children like you?
- How are each of your children like their other parent?
- How are each of your children like one another?

- How are each of your children different from one another?

What are you doing right as a parent?

- What do you believe you could have done better or wish you had done differently as a parent?

#210 - GIVING BIRTH

Write a letter to each of your children describing your feelings on the day of their birth

#211 - YOUR CHILD'S LANDMARK

Write your memories of a landmark event in the lives of your children

Here are some suggestions

- Potty training
- Your child's first day of school
- Your child's first win and first loss
- Your child's first injury or illness
- The first time your child slept over at a friend's house
- Your child's first kiss
- When you told your child about sex and "the facts of life"
- When your child got a driver's license
- First time your child traveled away from home without the family
- Your child's first home away from the family home
- When your child left home to go to college or marry
- When your child gave birth to your grandchildren

#212 - YOUR CHILD'S SCAR

What is the story behind your child's first scar?

- How did you feel the first time your child had an injury that left a scar?

#213 - YOUR CHILD'S HEALTH

Describe any serious illness or injury experienced by your child

- What happened?
- Was your child hospitalized?

Was there any permanent disability or scarring as a result of this illness or injury?

- How did your child deal with this change?
- What impact did this change have on you and your family members?

#214 - PARENTING LOSS

Have you lost a child through death or estrangement?

- What happened?

How did you cope with your loss?

#215 - NON-PARENTING

If you never had children, why not?

- You never wanted children
- You wanted children but it was never the "right time"
- There were physical or biological impediments to having children
- You never met the person with whom you wanted to have children
- Or?

If you did not have children, do you have a "substitute"?

- Niece, nephew, or Godchild
- A friend's child
- Pet

If you did not have children, do you now regret that decision?

#216 - LOSS OF A TREASURED THING

Was something you treasured ever lost or destroyed? How?

- A physical object
- Something intangible such as a friendship

Were you able to re-create or regain this thing or was it lost forever?

- Was the re-created or regained thing better or worse than the original?

Did you cause this loss, or was it caused by someone or something else?

- If you caused the loss, do you now wish you had kept this thing?

How did this loss impact you?

- How did you recover from your loss?
- Did you forgive the person or thing causing the loss?

#217 - FAMILY FEUDS

Is there a feud between members of your family?

What caused it?

- Estate or inheritance
- Judgments and misunderstandings about an issue or action
- Money
- Feeling that you were not appreciated
- Unequal treatment of siblings by parents
- Conflicts and misunderstandings between parents and children
- Jealousy
- Obligations not shared equally among family members
- Family members taking sides against one another
- Conflicts simmering since childhood
- It's not really a feud, you just have nothing in common
- Or?

Was there a reconciliation?

- How did it come about?

If there was no reconciliation, do you believe that the estrangement is permanent?

- What can you do to bring peace to your family?
- Do you want to bring peace and reconciliation to your family, but feel there is no hope?

What is your perspective of the feud?

Loss of Something Treasured
by Sallie Ringle

It's 26 years now. This loss has cut into me deeply. You see my loss is of my brother. He did not die. He stopped having a relationship with me. For over 20 years he has refused to speak to me. I was never allowed a relationship with my nephews, and knew only what my mother shared with me. This was especially hard for me because my brother is my only sibling.

I will explain the circumstances which brought about this loss. In the fall of 1989, I got a call from my brother in Maine asking if I would be willing to look after his wife's great-uncle if they sent him down to Florida for the winter. At the time I was working cleaning houses, helping some elderly manage their homes, going to college, and taking care of my own family. But I said, "Yes of course." Uncle Ozzie would pay me a small amount for my trouble.

Uncle Ozzie was to stay at a motel with long-term stay accommodations. He would need me to take him grocery shopping, do his laundry, and check up on him. I found him to be completely delightful. He had a few strange behaviors, but I figured they were because he was born in 1900.

I really involved Uncle Ozzie in our family life. I would bring him home for dinner. He and I would go on little adventures together. As a family we took him to church with us occasionally. Uncle Ozzie would ask me why I was so good to him, and I replied that I really liked him and that it was my Christian obligation to serve others.

In the spring of 1990, his niece came down from Maine and stayed for a week. Uncle Ozzie got sick after she left and was hospitalized. I realized he was not well enough to go back to his motel apartment, and brought him to live with my family. He was with us for six weeks before I was to fly him back to Maine. Now you need to understand that Uncle Ozzie was very much intact mentally. He was on constant oxygen and a special diet which I followed rigorously plus a boatload of medicine which I managed.

The end of May it was arranged for me to fly him home to Maine. I made arrangements to have an oxygen machine delivered to the hotel in Bangor so it would be there when we arrived. I was concerned that he would not have oxygen while we were actually traveling, but he was OK.

There was a little catch. In one of the phone calls Uncle Ozzie made from my house, he had made arrangements for his New York lawyer to meet him in Bangor. I knew nothing about this until we were at the hotel and he told me. He made me promise not to tell on him because his family wouldn't let him talk to his lawyer, and this was the only way he could do it. After I had seen how his niece treated him the week she was in Florida, I believed him. I stayed away while the consultations were going on between Uncle Ozzie and his lawyer.

The family found out about this meeting when they arrived in Bangor. They were hopping mad. My sister-in-law yelled at me. Her mother was furious and accused me of all sorts of ugly things. The truth was I knew nothing about what went on with the lawyer. The six days I spent in Maine with my brother and his family were some of the worst days of my life.

About a month after I got home, I got a call from my father saying he was coming to see me and had something important to discuss. Dad lived in California and I was in Florida, and I couldn't imagine what was so important he would fly all the way out to see me.

Well, it was important. Uncle Ozzie had died about ten days after I took him home. When he met with his lawyer, he had changed his will. He had taken out an inheritance to a deceased niece's husband. The money that was to go to this man was now to go to me. I knew nothing of this. That started the family feud. My brothers-in-law sued me and I had to go to New York City to appear at trial. The first day of the trial the judge threatened my brother's family with jail for tampering with the mail. They had opened Uncle Ozzie's mail from the law office and found out what he had done. In the end the judge told the lawyers to make a settlement and not come back to court until it was finalized.

I agreed to settle for half of the amount left to me. The lawyer would get a third of that. In the end it wasn't enough to have lost my only brother over. It is said that there are no wars worse than families fighting over money. I have found that to be so true. I know that I am innocent of having any part in the changes to the will. I think Uncle Ozzie was so happy and thankful for what I did for him that he wanted to do this for me. If I had known what he was doing I might have told him that he shouldn't include me in his will.

About five years ago my brother started to talk to me because our mother began failing. He will only talk to me about her. He has come to California several times and is cordial, but not caring or loving. That part of our lives is dead. It makes me so sad. I know that once Mother dies I will never have contact with my brother again. This is a loss I will never get over.

#218 - MENDING

Do you have fences to mend or things to say in order to make peace with yourself or others?

- What would you say or do to mend those fences?

#219 - ABUNDANCE

Abundance is about being rich, with or without money.

- SUZE ORMAN -

He has achieved success who has lived well, laughed often, and loved much.

- ELBERT GREEN HUBBARD -

What gives you feelings of abundance?

- How can you achieve abundance?

What does abundance mean to you?

- Family and friends
- Faith
- Money and possessions
- Love
- Happiness
- Beauty
- Creativity
- Or?

#220 - SINS

The traditional seven deadly sins are wrath, greed, sloth, pride, lust, envy, and gluttony.

What are your personal deadly sins?

HELPFUL HINT #24

FILE THINGS AWAY

As times goes by, family stories may go from hurtful to interesting. My great-grandfather immigrated to America as a teenager to avoid conscription into the army of the Austro-Hungarian Empire. If told too close to the event, this makes my great-grandfather sound like a draft-dodger who shirked his duty, and may be hurtful. But many years have passed since my great-grandfather's death, and his story has become an interesting part of my family's history and no longer has the power to wound.

If you have stories you want to preserve as an important part of your family's history but do not want to include them in your memoir, write them down and put them away in a file to be opened later when your family is ready to hear them or after you are gone. You may want to do this with things you believe could be hurtful or damaging if told now, but that your family should know as part of their history. Write these things down, file them away, and let them be read by future generations when they are interesting and quaint and can no longer cause hurt.

Remember though, sometimes a secret is not yours to tell. Your memoir is not the place to violate confidences or express your feelings of rancor or animosity toward others. You do not want to be remembered as a thoughtless person who violated the privacy of others.

#221 - WEIRD

Describe the most outlandish, weird, or bizarre thing that happened to you

#222 - SOMETHING SAID

Has someone said just one thing to you that changed your life?

- What was said?
- Who said it?

Was this a good piece of advice or a negative comment?

How did it change your life?

- Was the result of this change positive or negative?

#223 - YOUR HERO

Describe the traits and characteristics of a superhero you create

- What is the name of your superhero?

What is the form of your superhero?

- Human
- Animal or insect
- Mechanical or robotic
- Extra-terrestrial
- Fantasy figure
- Crusading champion of the people
- Sorcerer or wizard
- Enchantress or siren
- Or?

How are you like your superhero?

#224 - SPECIAL

To whom are you special?

- Parents, siblings, grandparents, other relatives
- Spouse
- Your children and grandchildren
- Job mentor
- Best friend
- Neighbor
- Teacher, counselor, coach
- Spiritual or religious leader
- Or?

What makes you special to this person?

- Love
- Family relationships
- Friendship
- Shared interests or a common cause
- Shared history and background

- Respect
- Or?

What does this special relationship mean to you?

- Has the nature of this relationship changed over time?

Has this relationship been a factor in your decision-making?

- Advice you've been given
- Having a chance to talk things over
- Looking to this person as a role model
- Wanting this person to think well of you
- Or?

#225 - HEIRLOOM

Do you have any family heirlooms?

- What are the family stories of these heirlooms?
- Do you have any photos showing your family members using these heirlooms?

If you could choose one family heirloom to be yours, what would it be?

- Jewelry
- Furniture
- Artwork
- Silver
- Family letters or other documents
- Or?

Why did you choose this particular heirloom?

- What is the history of this item in your family?

If there are no family heirlooms, what items of yours do you want to pass down to your family that will become their heirlooms?

- What about your belongings will your family treasure?

#226 - RECIPE

What is your favorite recipe?

- How did you learn to make this recipe?
- Did you invent this recipe?
- Have you shared this recipe with others?

#227 - UNIQUE (1)

What makes your family unique?

#228 - UNIQUE (2)

What makes you unique?

6

HELPFUL HINT #25

BE TRUSTWORTHY

There is a difference between storytelling and telling your story.

- LUCERNE HAMER -

This is your story, and you are entitled to tell it from your point of view. Part of the reason for telling your story is that you have things you want to say, and not just repeat the beliefs, philosophies, or experiences of others.

Your perception of events is authentic to you because it's your opinion and your viewpoint. But remember, your beliefs may be based on false interpretations, misunderstandings, or faulty memory. You may not always remember events accurately, but you need to be trustworthy. Record what you honestly believe occurred, but don't embellish facts to prove your point, and don't lie.

#229 - OUTDOORS

Write your memories of the "great outdoors"

- What is the most beautiful thing you have ever seen in nature?
- What outdoor adventure left you in awe?

Was there ever a time when you were frightened by the natural world?

- Did this experience make you reluctant to pursue other outdoor activities?

#230 - MOMENT

Describe your Big Moment

#231 - CHARITY

Are you a charitable person?

What are your special causes?

- Children
- Education
- Environment
- Animals
- Religion
- Health related issues
- Or?

Why is this charity of special interest to you?

- It represents part of your core values and beliefs
- You read or heard something about this charity that touched you
- You or someone close to you had a personal experience, such as an illness, that led to your interest in this charity
- This charity helped you when you needed help, and you want to give back
- Your support of this charity honors the memory of a loved one

#232 - LET ME HELP

Describe any volunteer work you do or regular donations your make

- As a teen
- As an adult
- Now

What are your areas of interest?

- School, literacy, education related activities
- Religious activities
- Scouting
- Rotary, Junior League, other community assistance organizations
- Environmental or conservation groups
- Fraternal organizations such as Masons or Elks
- Healthcare or disease prevention
- Political activism
- Children
- Animals
- Athletics
- Or?

How have your areas of interest changed as you aged?

- What caused this change?

#233 - ANGEL

How have you been an angel in the life of another?

- What is the best or nicest thing you did for another person?

If it is hard for you to sing your own praises, describe a situation in which someone was an angel to you.

#234 - CRUELTY

Describe something said to you or something you said that you find difficult to forgive or forget

- A time when you said or did something cruel, even if it was unintentional
- A time when someone said or did something cruel to you, even if it was unintentional

How did you deal with what was said to you?

Does it still hurt?

- How do you cope with your memory of this cruelty?

HELPFUL HINT #26

WATCH YOUR WORD CHOICE

You want to write with your authentic voice, but confrontational, abusive, or offensive language and using words solely for their shock value may be inappropriate, and make your readers dislike you. In a conversation, if you said, "Fuck you, John," then using that language is appropriate because it gives your readers a true sense of the intensity of your emotions. Choose words for their effectiveness so you communicate precisely what you mean to say. Don't use words in a way that is so offensive it makes your readers dislike you and your story.

Of course, you need to be careful that you don't lose your memoir's impact through over-sanitation. "A bear shit in the woods," is much more effective than, "The ursine creature defecated in the undergrowth."

Remember though, a little bear poop goes a long way.

#235 - DON'T LIKE THAT PERSON (1)

Describe someone you do not like

- The dullest person you ever met
- The meanest person you ever met
- The cruelest person you ever met

Why do you dislike this person?

- Is there a rational reason for your dislike?

#236 - DON'T LIKE THAT PERSON (2)

Are there any people you don't like or love but feel you should?

- What happened to make you feel this way?

Why do you feel obligated to like or love this person?

- Family relationships
- Job relationships

- Neighbors
- Members of your faith community
- Relatives or friends of your friends
- Or?

#237 - PAIN

I didn't think I would ever get over this

- Death of a loved one
- A missed opportunity
- A serious illness or injury
- Sad memories
- An abusive childhood
- Lost love
- An abandonment
- An emotional or physical attack
- Or?

But you're still here and you survived

- How did you learn to live with your pain?
- What did you have to do to become a survivor?

#238 - COMPASSION

When do you feel compassion?

How do you show compassion?

- For people
- For animals
- For the world

#239 - KINDNESS

Describe a random act of kindness

- Something you did for someone else
- Something someone did for you
- An unexpected kindness from a casual acquaintance or stranger

Cancer and Kindness

by Ann Hamer

In November 1998, after a mammogram, ultrasound, and excisional biopsy, I was diagnosed with breast cancer. I was a student, and had very little money and no health insurance. All the testing to determine I had cancer was paid for by the state of California through a special breast cancer testing initiative, but after I was diagnosed, my choice seemed to be either death or debt. It took two months and many phone calls to find a way to fund my treatment. I was finally scheduled to have a mastectomy in February 1999.

At the time, I was renting the upstairs of Marsha's house while she lived downstairs. Marsha had become a good friend, and although she had plans to go to Monterey the weekend before my mastectomy, she offered to stay home to provide encouragement and many glasses of wine prior to Monday's surgery. I told her to go ahead with her plans because my friend Tracy had promised to come to Upland and spend the weekend with me.

On Friday, just a few hours before Tracy was due to arrive, she phoned and said she was not coming. She wanted to work that weekend, her cat was sick, and her boyfriend's parents were in town. I told her I was hurt. She had promised, I relied on her promise, and Marsha had gone off to Monterey. I told Tracy she could work any time, and to tell her boyfriend to take care of the cat and make her excuses to his parents. Tracy responded by absolutely BLASTING me. She said she was a good friend, a good girlfriend, a good daughter, a good sister, and a good employee. (And presumably a good cat owner, although she did not say so.) I had to understand. Then she hung up.

I started crying. I was going to be mutilated in less than three days, Tracy had backed out on me and Marsha had gone to Monterey - because I said it was OK to do so. Mom would have come - she and Dad were planning to come for the surgery anyway - but even though I love Mom a lot, sometimes she is just way too motherly. I wanted to make jokes and laugh and be silly and eat lots of sugar. I wanted a friend.

I had a friend from school, Patty, who I thought I might be able to ask. I was hesitant because she was married and worked two part-time jobs, so her weekends were always busy. She knew about my cancer, and at my "Say good-bye to Ann's left breast" party, she had written and sung two songs for me, one of which included the immortal line, "Now that you're a one-breasted woman, you'll have to find a one-handed man."

I called Patty. I apologized. I said I knew it was last minute, and I was sorry to ask, but could she, would she, please come to Upland and spend some time with me. She responded with absolutely no hesitation and said, "I'll be there. I'll be there for as long as you need me to be there." And she was. And it meant everything to me - because she surprised me with her kindness, because she did not hesitate, and because she just came.

Patty and I were school friends - we had classes together, hung out on campus, ate out a few times with other friends, had fun together. Until this happened, I would have considered her a good friend, but not one of my closest friends. But she stepped up for me, and I'll never forget it.

It has been many years since my mastectomy. I am cancer-free. Patty and I lost touch, and I have not seen her for a long time. Tracy called my mom after my surgery to ask how I was doing. I spoke with her when I got home from the hospital to tell her I was fine. I later wrote Tracy telling her how hurt I was and that I wanted to stay friends, but things had to change. I was tired of arranging our get-togethers and driving long distances to see her, only to have her give me just an hour of her time because she had to go to the gym or hit a bucket of golf balls or knit an afghan. I showed the letter to Marsha. She said it was a good letter and not unkind, it just stated what I needed. Marsha also said I should not be surprised if Tracy did not reply. She was right - I never heard from Tracy again.

I now live with my mom, and Marsha and I are still good friends.[1]

#240 - BLESSING

Whom do you want to bless?

- What are your words of blessing?

#241 - HOORAY FOR ME

What do you like about yourself?

---

1   I read this story to my writers group. They asked if I knew where Patty was, and when I said yes, encouraged me to send this story to her. I did, and we got back in touch and are close friends once again. Wonderful things can happen when you write the story of your life!

#242 - NEXT

What's next?

#243 - HOBBIES

What are your hobbies?

- As a child?
- As a busy young adult?
- In middle age?
- Now?

Do you still pursue the hobbies you had when you were younger?

- If you don't, would you like to?
- Do you think you will?

If you no longer pursue these hobbies, why did you lose interest?

#244 - COLLECTING

What did you collect?

- As a child
- As a young adult
- In middle age
- Now

Why did you collect these things?

- What about them attracted you?

Do you still collect these things?

- If you do not, why did you stop?
- What did you do with your collection?

#245 - OOPS

"Why did I ever buy . . ."

It seemed like a good idea at the time, but it just didn't turn out the way I planned

- Too expensive

- It didn't look right once you got it home
- You didn't use it
- It did not live up to your expectations
- Or?

#246 - FUN

What do you do for fun?

- How do you feel when you are unable to do fun things?

#247 - CURRENT INTERESTS

What are you interested in right now?

- Studying a particular event or historical era
- Politics
- Going to school or taking classes
- Working toward graduation
- A special person
- Parenting
- Religion
- Health
- Your job or finding a new career
- Retirement
- New recipes
- New love
- Learning a new skill
- Pursuing an old skill
- Finding old friends
- Making new friends
- Mending relationships
- Something you once said you'd do if you had the time
- Creating art
- Caring for a loved one
- Your hobby
- Or?

HELPFUL HINT #27

BEWARE OF YOUR POWER TO WOUND

After my father retired, he took writing classes at the local senior center. His stories told of his childhood, marriage, family, and career. In all of my father's stories I, his only daughter, was mentioned just once, and then not by name, but only as my brothers' sister. (My brothers were in many of his stories and always mentioned by name.) Even though my father is now deceased, this omission still hurts.

Remember you are writing your memoir for others to read, and you do not want your tone to be hurtful, spiteful, or angry. You do not want to omit people - your children, your spouse, your parents, or other family members - unless there is an estrangement and you have a valid reason for the omission. If there is an estrangement, it is part of your story and should be explained.

Check to see if you are wounding others by having a trusted but disinterested person read your memoir and tell you honestly how it sounds. This reader should not be a family member or someone mentioned in your stories.

#248 - BELIEVE IT OR NOT

"You may not believe it, but this really happened to me"

- Describe what happened
- What made it so unbelievable?

#249 - TRAVEL

Where have you traveled?

- Where is the most exciting place you visited?

Who were your traveling companions?

- Do you like to travel alone or with others?

What is your favorite mode of transportation when you travel?

- Plane
- Car or motorcycle
- Train
- Cruise ship, river boat, canoe, or kayak

- Walking or hiking
- Bicycle
- Horse
- Or?

#250 - DARING TRAVEL

What is the most daring or adventurous thing you've done while traveling?

- Have you ever been in danger or threatened while traveling?

#251 - SPECIAL TRAVEL

Have you traveled to that one special place you've always wanted to see?

- What was it about this place that attracted you?

Did your experience live up to your expectations?

- Did visiting this place change your life in any way?
- Was this change positive or negative?

#252 - VACATION

Describe your vacations

- Favorite vacation
- Most disappointing vacation
- Vacation that was better than you expected

Describe your perfect vacation

- Where is it?
- What would you do when you got there?
- Who would you go with?
- Have you actually been on this vacation or is it a dream or fantasy?

Describe your best and worst days on vacation

#253 - LESS TRAVELED

In his poem "The Road Not Taken", Robert Frost wrote, "I took the one less traveled by, and that has made all the difference."

When and how have you taken the road less traveled?

- When did you zig when you could have zagged?

How did it make a difference?

- What were the positive and negative impacts of your decision?

Was there a time when you did not take the road less traveled? Why not?

- You weren't brave enough
- You did what was expected, rather than what you wanted
- You like the well-traveled road
- Or?

How did *not* taking the road less traveled make a difference?

- What were the positive and negative impacts of your decision?

#254 - FRIENDSHIP (1)

New friends may be poems, but old friends are alphabets.
Do not forget the alphabets because you will need them to read the poems.

- AUTHOR UNKNOWN -

Who was your best friend as a child, as an adult, and now?

- Are you still in contact with the best friend you had as a child?

If you don't have a best friend, why not?

- Don't want one
- Don't need one
- Haven't found one
- Don't want people getting too close to me
- I have lots of friends, but none I consider the "best"

If you don't have a best friend, how has this impacted you?

#255 - FRIENDSHIP (2)

What qualities do you value most in a friend?

- What qualities do you value most in the friends you have now?
- What qualities did you value most in the friends you had as a child?

How are you a good friend?

HELPFUL HINT #28

BE OPEN

It's hard to be objective about your own writing. For a long time I thought *everything* I wrote was wonderful. Then I re-read my writings and thought everything I wrote was terrible. Now my opinion is more balanced. Some of my writing is good, some is bad, and some of it contains good ideas but needs more work.

Don't get too attached to the way you tell your story or to your writing style. You want your writing to reflect your true voice, but if you become overly attached, you will be deaf to good advice that may help improve your story.

#256 - YOU CAN'T PLEASE EVERYONE

Has someone ever just not liked you?

- How did that make you feel?

Did you try to get this person to like you?

- Were your efforts successful?

What were the negative impacts of this person's dislike?

- Employer or boss who did not like you
- Teacher or coach who did not like you
- Club president or advisor who did not like you
- Relative who did not like you
- Former friend who later disliked you
- Or?

How did you deal with this rejection?

#257 - PEOPLE FROM YOUR PAST

"I wonder whatever happened to ..."

- Have you lost contract with someone who was once an important part of your life and now wonder where they are?

Have you tried to find this person?

If you got in contact, what happened?

- Friendship renewed
- No longer any basis for a friendship, and nothing happened
- Or?

#258 - TRUST (1)

Whom do you trust?

- What did this person do to earn your trust?

#259 - TRUST (2)

Whom do you not trust?

- What did this person do to merit your distrust?

#260 - EXPLANATION

Write a letter explaining yourself to someone you have not seen for a long time

#261 - TRIBUTE

Write a tribute to a friend

Thank You Carol

by Maria C.

The second week of February was a tough time. February 14th I received an email from Anita, my former classmate, announcing the death of her husband Scott. The next day, another email from our school website came with the news that Dely's husband died after his bypass surgery. Then the most devastating news. Carol, our good friend, died on February 16th. I was not expecting this tragic news. We had just seen Carol in April of the previous year.

My college friends, Cecilia, Tina, Marissa, and I decided to go to Las Vegas for "special bonding days". Cecilia and I live in Los Angeles. Tina lives in Switzerland, and every year stays in California from November to March to escape the harsh Swiss winter. Marissa, a New Jersey resident, visits Los Angeles to spend time with her best friend, Tina. Cecilia and I hadn't seen Marissa since graduation, and were eager to see her again.

On our first day, while we were having dessert at our hotel's coffee shop, Tina kept checking her watch. She would often leave the group to take a personal call on her cell phone. Finally we found out why Tina was so restless. She wanted to surprise us with the arrival of three more college friends. Before we could finish dessert, we saw walking toward our table Boots, Becky, and Lina. Boots and Becky both live in Vegas, and Lina, a resident of Vancouver, flew in to join our mini reunion.

As we were planning our itinerary, Boots said we should take time to visit Carol. She also lived in Vegas, and the sad news was that Carol had terminal cancer. Boots would call to schedule our visit. Carol would let us know if she could see us, depending on how she felt that day. On our second day we received a call from Carol. She was feeling well and could see us.

We didn't know what to expect. After all, it's not every day you visit a terminally ill friend you haven't seen in decades. When we arrived at her place, Carol was standing by the entrance door. She'd lost a lot of weight, looked frail and gaunt, but still had that "tall and stately" bearing from our college years. Her once long wavy hair was cropped short and almost totally gray.

Carol warmly welcomed us to her cozy home. She had wine and cheese and a variety of finger foods prepared for us. Once we were seated, each one of us gave an update of our lives since graduation. When it was Carol's turn, she calmly told us she had advanced and terminal cancer. She talked openly about it, and even told us how many months the doctors gave her. Carol gave us all these details to answer the questions we might be hesitant to ask.

It was a bewitching afternoon. Each one of us brought up funny incidents in college, and we talked about other college friends and former professors. There was indeed wild, deafening, boisterous laughter from all of us. We completely transformed ourselves to our "young college girls" persona. All of us forgot the sad fact we were there to see our terminally ill friend Carol. For her part, Carol was just like one of us - loud, animated, and intense - especially when discussing political issues in Las Vegas. If you didn't know her condition, you would never guess she was someone in the last stages of life.

After almost three hours, we could sense Carol was getting tired. Our group bade her goodbye with tight hugs and embraces. The seven of us knew this might be the last time we'd see our dear friend Carol. There was sadness about her as she saw us off and waved goodbye. I'm sure it also crossed her mind this might be the last time for her to see us. As we drove off, most of us looked one more time through the rear window just to catch a last glimpse of Carol, still standing by the door. We were all quiet and subdued as we drove back to our hotel.

The day we heard the sad news of Carol's death, Cecilia, Tina, and I exchanged long emails mourning the death of our dear friend. We all shared the same sentiment: that we were lucky and blessed to have seen Carol that April afternoon. The three of us treasured in our hearts that precious bonding time we spent with our dear friend Carol.

Carol was a courageous woman who didn't let cancer defeat her. She knew her days were numbered but this didn't stop her from living life to the fullest. That April afternoon our group learned a valuable lesson. Carol taught us that it is okay to accept your fate, be at peace with yourself, and most of all embrace what lies ahead. Carol was ready to let go of her earthly home and move on to her eternal home. She was one brave lady!

Rest in peace Carol, our dear friend. You will always be in our thoughts and prayers.

#262 - COMMUNITY

What does community mean to you?

- Where you live
- Family and friends
- Like-minded people
- Common religious traditions or beliefs
- Common cause
- Club
- Or?

How do you benefit your community?

- Host family meals
- Provide financial support or make donations
- Attend meetings
- Volunteer your time
- Write letters
- Provide food and shelter
- And?

How is community important to you?

- Do you have many different communities?

#263 - TEACHING

How are you a teacher?

- Whom do you teach?
- What do you teach?

#264 - ENCOURAGEMENT

From whom did you receive the most encouragement?

- What did this person say or do to encourage you?

#265 - INSPIRATION/PERSPIRATION

Genius is one percent inspiration and ninety-nine percent perspiration.

-THOMAS EDISON-

Who or what gives you inspiration?

- What makes you perspire?

How do your inspiration and perspiration work together to help you succeed?

HELPFUL HINT #29

USE CONTEMPORARY LANGUAGE

Make your story real to your readers by using words and phrases popular during the time about which you are writing.

Pat Beauchamp served with the First Aid Nursing Yeomanry in France and Belgium during the First World War. She was from the British upper class, and knew very little about doing practical things. Notice how this short excerpt from her story, published in 1919, effectively captures the time, place, and personality of the writer.

Before Bridget left, she explained how I was to light the Primus stove ... When the time came, I put the mentholated in the little cup at the top, lit it, and then pumped with a will. The result was a terrific roar and a sheet of flame reaching almost to the roof! Never having seen one in action before, I thought it was possible they always behaved like that at first and that the conflagration would subside in a few moments. I watched it doubtfully, arms akimbo. Bridget entered just then, and determined not to appear flustered, in as cool a voice as possible I said, "Is that all right old thing?" She put down her parcels and, without a word, seized the stove by one of its legs and threw it on a sand heap outside! Of course the stove had gone out ... and I felt I was not the brightest jewel I might have been.

- PAT BEAUCHAMP WASHINGTON -

#266 - MIRROR

What do you see when you look in the mirror?

- Your own image
- The thing over your shoulder
- Something on the other side
- Or?

#267 - MOTHERS

You may find this exercise difficult and very emotional. Even when memories of your mother are happy, there may still be sadness because the experiences you had with your mother are now over, and will not happen again. With one's mother - mine, yours, anyone's - there is bound to be longing for what you had, thoughts about what you wish had been, regrets, happiness, joy, sorrow, grief, anger, laughter - you name it - the whole range of emotions.

If you find writing about your mother too difficult, try writing about you as a mother. It doesn't have to be about mothering your own children. You can write about giving motherly advice to someone. You can write about mothering animals, or about doing something for someone else's mother. I have a wonderful mother and love her dearly, but when I did this exercise, I wrote about a time when I had the privilege and honor of being asked to "mother" a friend at the end of her life.

Although this prompt is called "Mothers", it is actually about the person who nurtured you, no matter who that person may be. As you write your response, think about the person who was the nurturing presence in your life. Remember, "mothering" is not limited to women with children. "Mothering" is not limited to women. It is about nurturing, and everyone has the ability to "mother" when they nurture and care.

Write a Mother's Day message

You may write a message to

- Your mother (or the mother figure) who raised you
- A friend who acted as a mother to you
- The mother of your children or grandchildren
- Someone who gave you motherly advice
- The mother you wish you had
- The person who nurtured you
- Yourself

Here are some suggestions

- Write about a Mother's Day card or gift you gave to your mother
- Write about a Mother's Day card or gift you received from your children or grandchildren
- Write the Mother's Day card you wish you had sent to your mother or the person who nurtured you
- Write the Mother's Day card you wish you had received from your children
- Write about a time you were mothered or nurtured when you really needed it
- Write about a time you mothered or nurtured someone who really needed it

The Red Shoes

by Susan Fraizer

It was my fifth birthday. My grandfather, Carlo Aluffo Charles, was taking me shopping for a new outfit. That was something we didn't get very often. A lot of our clothes were second hand, which was alright because they were clean and presentable. But I knew I was going to a dress store for a new outfit. I was so excited! We went to a children's dress shop in Alhambra, California. Grandpa and I went in and he asked for a saleslady to help us.

I remember walking among rows of beautiful dresses. They were fancy dresses with lace on the edge of beautiful sheer fabric. The underlining was silky fabric and so soft. I loved the pink dresses. That was the color I wanted. I picked the style I wanted and the saleslady brought everything in my size. I had a new slip, panties, white socks with lace trim, and a beautiful pale pink dress with little white dots on it, as soft as velvet. It was the most beautiful dress that was ever mine at the age of five.

Now it was time to pick out my new shoes. We went over to the shoe department and looked at all the shoes. It was almost overwhelming to know that I could have new shoes too. I spotted the exact pair I wanted. They were a beautiful red pair with a strap across the instep. I thought they were irresistible. I told the saleslady they were the shoes I wanted. She told me they were red and did not go with my new pink dress. I didn't understand it. I had the prettiest pink dress. Why not have the prettiest red shoes to go with it? The saleslady didn't want to give in. She said they just didn't go together. Grandpa stepped into the conversation. He told the saleslady that if his granddaughter wanted red shoes with her pink dress, that was what she was going to have. The next thing I knew I was being fitted for my new red shoes. I was so happy.

Next my Grandpa did the most wonderful thing. I was all dressed up and ready to go. There were these long tables, maybe three in a row. They were empty. He picked me up so I could stand on this "runway". He held my hand and walked me all the way down the tables singing, "Here she comes, Miss America," as loudly as he could. Everybody turned and watched as I finished my walk. He helped me down from the table and we walked out of the store.

What a glorious day it was. I have never forgotten the way he could make me feel so special.

#268 - SURPRISE (1)

What do people not know about you that may surprise them?

#269 - SURPRISE (2)

Write about a time when you were surprised

#270 - VALUES

What are your most deeply held values?

- What values are an integral part of the person you are?

Was there ever a time when your values were challenged?

- How did you respond to the challenge?
- Did your values waver or change?

How have your most deeply held values changed as you've aged?

- What values did you have as a child, teenager, and young adult that you no longer hold?
- Why did your values change?

HELPFUL HINT #30

HANG IN THERE

The memoir writing process can be hard, and may bring up many emotions. Part of the process is becoming comfortable with telling *your* story in *your* way with *your* voice. Speaking with your true voice is part of your legacy. The story of your life deserves to be told, and it deserves to be told as *you* want to tell it.

I hope you find the memoir writing experience meaningful, but as you write, you may find some things become emotional and very hard. Be nice to yourself. If something is too difficult, put it aside and come back to it later. Look at the things that make you smile, and put away the difficult things for another time. I promise you that the more you write, the easier it will get.

When you stay with it, even when it gets difficult, it says a lot about your strength and your perseverance. You and your readers will be richly rewarded by the peace you find and legacy you create when you write the story of your life.

#271 - BRAVERY

The world is a dangerous place to live; not because of the people who are evil,
but because of the people who don't do anything about it.

- ALBERT EINSTEIN -

When were you brave?

- Physical bravery
- Speaking up in support of someone or something unpopular
- Demonstrating the courage of your convictions
- Standing up to a bully

Did you ever speak up or take action when you saw something wrong?

- What did you say?
- What was the result?

Were you ever endangered or threatened while doing an act of bravery?

#272 - SHIPWRECK

If you were shipwrecked on a deserted island, what would you want to have with you?

- Electronic devices
- Cell phone
- Books

- Music and movies
- Writing materials
- Art and drawing materials
- Another person
- A companion animal
- A boat
- Or?

How long could you be on a deserted island before you'd want to return to civilization?

- No more than a few weeks
- Forever - I want to stay!

Don't be limited by logic. Assume you have enough food, water, clothing, sun screen, and shelter. Do not worry about bringing practical things to your island. This is an exercise in fantasy. Release your imagination and write!

#273 - ABANDON (1)

Were you ever forced to leave someone or something behind?

- An object
- A person
- A pet
- An attitude
- A memory
- Or?

How did this make you feel?

- Relieved
- Disappointed
- Sad or heartbroken
- Abandoned
- Empty or lost
- Or?

#274 - ABANDON (2)

Was there ever a time when you were abandoned or felt abandoned?

- Who abandoned you?
- What happened?

How did this make you feel?

- Hurt
- Rejected
- At a loss
- In danger
- Disappointed
- Or?

#275 - BLINDSIDED

Write about a time when you didn't see it coming

Movin' to California

by Micki Daniels

I was about nine years old when my fourth sister was born. I was the oldest of three sisters, and we were all so happy to have another baby in the house. But months went by and our baby sister just laid still, no moving, no crying, no nothing, so Mom said, "Something is not right with our baby." Mom and Dad took her to the doctor, and after some testing, it was discovered our baby was born with severe brain damage. What was once a home of laughing, playing, and fighting suddenly became a quiet sad home. Mom cried a lot and Dad drank more. My other sisters and I got closer together and helped Mom more. I was 14 years old when Mom and Dad sat us three girls down to tell us we had to move out of New York as the winters were so bad for our baby sister she would not survive another winter. So Mom in her kind way told us, "Go to your room and pick out five outfits you really like, two pairs of shoes, and seven pairs of panties and socks." We all looked at each other and somehow knew our life was about to change in a big way.

One day after the announcement, a lady came to our house and took our couch and chair. I asked Mom why the lady took our couch away, and she replied, "We are selling all our furniture and everything in the house so we can have money to move to California." I still remember when my bed and dresser came down the stairs, and a man and his son took them away in their truck.

Soon everything was gone, even the dishes, pots, pans, and silverware. One day Dad came home and said, "OK girls, come out and see your new home," and outside in our driveway was a silver bullet trailer and what to us, was a new car. Dad said, "This is how we are getting to California." Now when I think what my parents did, I say they were warriors. How brave of them to go across country with five kids (by now there were five sisters), and no job waiting for Dad.

We made it to Missouri when our car broke down. It was hot, and we were standing outside our trailer when a woman who lived up the hill from the gas station where Dad had stopped came over to Mom and said, "Come on Darlin' and bring all your babies up to my house for some cookies and lemonade." She had swings in her backyard, so while we ran around and played, Mom and this lady got acquainted. We were there all day until Dad could buy another car. When we left the lady said, "Goodbye girls. It was nice to meet such good girls." She hugged and kissed Momma goodbye and said, "God bless and good luck to you all." She was our angel on the road!!

After what seemed like an eternity, we finally arrived at the California border. The border agent asked if we had any fruit or vegetables, and Mom said, "Yes, I have five peaches." The agent said, "Sorry lady, you can't bring any fruit into California." Mom explained that the five peaches were her girls, and everyone had a good laugh. Soon Daddy found a job, and we sold the trailer and rented a nice house. I was 15, and there was an 18 year old girl who lived down the street. One day we walked to the top of the hill in front of my house. She asked if I wanted to smoke. I had never smoked but wanted to try, so I said yes.

She tried to light the cigarettes, but the wind kept blowing out the match. She threw the used matches on the ground, when suddenly we realized the hill was on fire!! I grabbed my jacket and hit at the flames. Big mistake - all that did was spread the fire. We ran down the hill for home. My heart was pounding so fast! Soon the fire department showed up and put out the fire. Then they came to my house. My dear mom did not know I had started the fire. She was adamant as she told the fireman, "Oh no, my girls would not do that!" The minute the fireman looked at me and asked if I was smoking on the hill, I could not tell a lie and started to cry and said, "Yes, it was me!"

The way he looked at me I thought for sure he was going to take me to jail! Mom, sensing my fear, told the fireman, "Thank you sir. I'll take care of this for now." Mom took the opportunity to teach us all a lesson. "OK girls - you see what smoking can do, so I never want you girls to smoke."

Lesson learned. None of us every smoked. As the saying goes, Momma was right!

#276 - BEYOND

What pain do you have that is beyond the power of love and forgiveness to heal?

#277 - ANSWERS

Why

- I did (or did not) get that job
- I did (or did not) get that part
- I did (or did not) get chosen for the team
- That person did (or did not) love me
- They forgot I was there

7

HELPFUL HINT #31

WRITE OUT NEGATIVITY

Memoir writing is sometimes a painful process. Whether you use a pen or your computer, the act of writing makes you pause and reflect. If you're a glass half empty sort of person, your tone may come across as hostile, bitter, or depressed. You don't want your written legacy to be one of anger or negativity.

Some of the exercises in this book may help you to write out your anger and your hurt. Write out your pain, and then throw it away or file it, and start over again. Keep writing until you find your true voice, free from any expressions of anger or frustration. You'll find the writing process cathartic, and as you find your true voice you may also find some peace.

#278 - ARTIST

How are you an artist?

We are all artists in some way, so describe how you are an artist, not if you are an artist.

#279 - POETRY

The vast majority of people find their only poetry in a good bellyful of food.

- HARRY KEMP -

Where do you find your poetry?

#280 - ONCE

Describe a time when once was enough

- Finding your one true love
- Taking the trip of a lifetime
- Surviving an illness or injury
- Something you just couldn't bear to do again
- Or?

#281 - CHANGE

Describe a single day or single incident that changed your life

- Birth of a child or grandchild
- Catastrophic accident, injury, illness
- First date
- Loss of a job or financial security
- The day you got the job
- Your first heartbreak
- Death of a loved one
- A chance meeting
- A time when you were lucky
- Your wedding day
- Or?

Hardship

by Robert Hamer

After 45 years of marriage, ten children, and fourteen hour work days, in 1935 my grandparents, Emma and William Brundle, were beginning to be rewarded. Their five surviving children had moved from the farm after World War I, and Will and Emma managed alone their eighty acres and a country store in rural Grape, Michigan.

One night a spark from the wood burning kitchen stove ignited the shingle roof. The building burned to the ground, destroying the store and attached living quarters. The only building to survive was the out-house. The two old people in their night clothes rescued each other, but no property was spared from the flames. My cousins and I later found a few pennies grossly bent by the heat, but everything else was gone.

Neighbors later described the red fireball that illuminated the night sky and the frantic efforts to save the property. The only fire truck was in Dundee, ten miles away. Everything burned: cherished photos of deceased children, furniture, store merchandise, truck, and heirlooms. What little cash Grandpa had accumulated was destroyed. Nothing survived and there was no insurance.

The Brundle conflagration was a tragic hardship, but Emma and Will recovered to celebrate their golden wedding anniversary. In my memory they were never cross with one another, never complained, and were never despondent. Their losses from the fire did not conquer my grandmother's humorous spirit or her loving authority over her husband, children, and grandchildren.

#282 - DESTINY

Do you believe you have (or had) a special destiny or purpose?

- Did you fulfill your destiny?

If you have not yet fulfilled your destiny, will you?

- What are you doing to fulfill your destiny?

#283 - PACKING (1)

If you had five minutes to pack a suitcase and leave your home, what would you take?

#284 - PACKING (2)

What things do you always pack to take on a trip?

#285 - INSIDER

Describe a time when you felt like an insider or a member of the "in" crowd

#286 - OUTSIDER

Describe a time when you felt like an outsider

#287 - ISOLATION

Describe a time when you were isolated

Describe a time when you felt isolated, even though you were not alone

#288 - CHEATED

Were you ever cheated out of something you deserved?

- A prize or award
- A raise or promotion
- An honor or commendation
- A scholarship
- An elected position
- Or?

Who cheated you?

Why do you think this happened?

- How did you react?

#289 - GOT AWAY

Describe the one that got away

- Love
- Job
- Opportunity

- A prize or scholarship
- Or?

Do you still think about the one that got away?

- How would your life have been different if it had not gotten away?

HELPFUL HINT #32

YOU'RE NOT ALWAYS THE HERO

You may be tempted to construct your story so that you are always the hero and always right. No one is perfect or always heroic, and no one always makes the right decisions. When you admit to making mistakes, you become more accessible and more likeable to your readers.

Your reader needs to trust that you are telling the truth. No one lives their life without making mistakes and doing some embarrassing things. You do not have to shamelessly strip yourself naked, and too many uncensored revelations could make your readers uncomfortable. But if you are not accurate in your self-portrayal, people may have doubts, will not trust you, and view you and your life story as works of fiction.

#290 - VIRAL

Write about a moment in your life that you hope won't go viral

#291 - OUT OF CONTROL

What are your addictions?

- Food
- Alcohol
- Drugs
- Gambling
- Shopping
- Sex
- Exercise
- Social media
- Online gaming
- Or?

How have your addictions impacted your life?

- Money issues
- Job loss
- Health issues
- Relationship loss
- Embarrassment
- Jail
- Harm caused to yourself or others
- Or?

#292 - BAD HABITS

Do you have any bad habits you can't seem to break?

- Procrastination
- Lazing in bed all day
- Wasting money
- Or?

How have your bad habits impacted your life?

#293 - WITHOUT

What did you not have while growing up that today most people take for granted?

- Indoor plumbing
- Television
- A private telephone line
- Your own room
- Privacy
- Financial security
- A car
- Pets
- Electronic devices and smart phones
- Social media and the internet
- And?

How did you feel when other people had the things that you did not?

- Envious
- Compelled to acquire the thing
- Happy for their good fortune
- Or?

How did you feel when you finally had this thing?

#294 - BULLY

Describe a time when you were bullied

Describe a time when you bullied another person

#295 - REVENGE

Have you ever been so angry you wanted to take revenge on someone?

- Who?
- What did this person do to make you want to take revenge?

Did you plot revenge?

- Did you carry out your plot?

Placing a Curse

by Barbara Cauthorn

Thoughts of homicide can occur even to peaceable, animal loving vegetarians. I have no experience with homicide, although I expect it's rather messy. I hate a mess, so maybe it's not a feasible course of action. I'm going to put a curse on him instead. By "him" I'm referring to my cousin. Co-beneficiary of his mother's estate. The estate I am the executor of. He is a person with no conscience.

An internet search reveals that, "Putting a curse on someone might cause you to enter a dark world of evil." No. Absolutely not. Another search suggests, "Send them love and forgiveness." No, that's not going to work either.

"A Simple Voodoo Hex Using Common Household Items." Ah! Just right. The goal is to foil someone's harmful plans, not to cause actual harm. Suggested targets are bullies, pain-in-the-neck neighbors, and intractable bigots.

I gathered cayenne pepper, tap water, candles, and a sturdy plastic bag. Then I wrote his name on a slip of paper. I waited for darkness and lit the candles. The cayenne pepper and a good slosh of water went into the bag, followed by the slip of paper. Securely seal the bag. We're ready to go.

Vigorously shake the bag like you're making cocktails. Stomp your feet forcefully.

"Open the Gate, spirits!" "Open the Gate!" "Jerry, I bind and confound your evil plans!!"

Continue stomping and shaking and yelling. Repeat until you feel that it's working. Thank the spirits and request them to close the Gate.

I blew out the candles, put the bag in the freezer (to be carefully disposed of later), and went to bed. It was my first good night's sleep in months.

A few days later, I began to itch. I'd recently returned from a road trip, and my first thought was, "Oh my god, bedbugs!" from highway motels. I stripped the bed, washed everything in hot water and bleach, vacuumed, inspected, washed and scrubbed some more. My goodness, my house was clean! Days went by. I still itched. I visited the walk-in clinic at the local Wal-mart.

"Dermatitis," he said. "My wife gets it, too. Every winter."

"I was afraid it was bedbugs," I said.

"Oh no," he said cheerfully, and wrote a prescription.

I'd never had dermatitis before. It's summer now and the itch has not gone away. If anything, it's gotten worse. I don't know what happened to my cousin. It's not like he confides in me.

#296 - WORTH

Describe an experience that was really worth it.

#297 - REGRET (1)

What are the "should haves" in your life?

- When you were young
- At mid-life
- Now

What is your biggest regret?

#298 - REGRET (2)

This above all: To thine own self be true.

- WILLIAM SHAKESPEARE -

Did you ever ignore your inside voice, and go ahead and do something that didn't feel quite right?

- Wrong job
- Wrong vacation
- Wrong spouse
- Wrong lover
- Wrong house
- Wrong school or university
- A criminal or dishonest activity
- Or?

What was the result?

- How would life have been different if you had listened to your inner voice?

#299 - DAYDREAM

What is your daydream?

- How have your daydreams changed as you've aged?

#300 - OTHER PEOPLE

If you could meet anyone - historical figure, celebrity, or ancestor - either living or dead, whom would you meet?

- What would you say to this person?
- What would you ask?

Why did you choose this person?

#301 - ADMIRATION

Write a letter to someone you admire

- What is it about this person that you admire?

Will you mail your letter?

HELPFUL HINT #33

SHOW DON'T JUST TELL

Engage your readers so they want to share your life. Don't just describe; help readers re-live your experiences with you. As you live through the events of your life, you don't know what will happen. You don't know if you'll get that job, get accepted to that school, survive that surgery, or accept that proposal. We don't know what will eventually happen as we live our daily lives. Try to bring that sense of anticipation and the unknown to your story.

Don't stand apart from your writing and your experiences. Bring emotion and sensation into your story to make it come alive. Describe not only what you saw, but also what you felt, smelled, heard, and tasted. Set the scene: the smell of a holiday, the taste of that first kiss, the feel of a beloved pet's head under your hand.

Put yourself into the action by avoiding passive language that distances you from the story. Write, "I know," rather than "It is known," or "I believe," rather than "It is generally believed."

Above all else, write from your heart!

#302 - HEART

Hold your heart in your hand. Create a small handmade heart: a paper heart, a felt heart, a heart you make from craft materials, or find a rock that looks like a heart, and then decorate it.

Write about your heart

- Feeling heart
- Healing heart
- Compassionate heart

- Loving heart
- Sacred heart
- Grieving heart
- Broken heart
- Parental heart
- Patient heart
- Overflowing heart
- Giving heart
- Shattered heart
- The heart you wear on your sleeve

How large is your heart?

- How can you make your heart grow larger?

How does it feel to hold your heart in your hand?

#303 - LOVE IN A BOX

Find a box or other container to hold your love.

What will you put in your box to fill it with love?

- The love you give to others
- The things you love about yourself
- The love you need from others
- Something tangible such as a card, ring, or gift from a loved one
- Your faith and spiritual beliefs
- Romance
- Friendship
- Kindness
- Forgiveness
- Laughter
- Memories
- Acceptance
- Time together
- Future love
- A loving pet
- Or?

Dear Little Sister

by Blanca Diaz

I'm sending you this box filled with all of the things that I know you will need for the next phase of your journey. I know things feel uncertain and you don't yet know where this new phase will lead you, but I know God will guide you.

Enclosed you will find the memories I have of our childhood along with all the things I remember that helped us get through it.

Resilience: You were never the giving up type, even when you fell off your bike you never gave up. Each scratch, bump and bruise you endured was a painful experience, but you still kept on trying. You would learn from it, dust yourself off, get up and try again.

Song: Listening to you sing always made me proud. Your voice can tell stories, it can make you cry and even dance. Don't forget to sing and dance along the way, otherwise we won't have a soundtrack!

Laughter: Your laughter helped me so much. I never thought I was funny, but your laughter gave me confidence and I thank you for that. Keep laughing, even right now when you feel like crying. We will soon laugh together and have better days. I promise.

Family: We are always here for you no matter what.

Love: Take love with you. Even a broken heart is better than no heart at all. I pray you will have the courage to love again.

Hope: There's always tomorrow. You never know what tomorrow will bring.

There might be some turbulence on the trip, but hang on! It's almost like when we were kids and we used to go to the fair. Remember those rides that always made us feel so sick? We always swore we would never get on them again, but we did it anyway. Love can be like that. And we always come out with a great story to tell.

I love you and hang in there. But most of all, enjoy the journey!

#304 - BROKEN HEART

Write about a time when your heart was broken

#305 - FANTASY (1)

Describe the fantasy you

- Royal or aristocrat
- President, political leader, diplomat
- Chef
- Spy
- Astronaut
- Explorer or world traveler
- Inventor or scientist
- Athlete
- Writer or best-selling author
- Actor or movie star
- Internet star
- Doctor or surgeon
- Teacher
- Parent
- Spouse
- Singer, musician, artist
- Rich person
- "Free spirit"
- Activist
- Or?

What attracts you about the idea of being this person?

- How are you like this person?

What would you do if you were this person?

#306 - FANTASY (2)

If you were on Fantasy Island, what would your fantasy be? Try to be specific about the details

- What are you doing?

- Who is with you?
- What is the era of your fantasy?
- What is the location of your fantasy?

What is it about living this fantasy that appeals to you?

- What does this fantasy tell you about yourself?

#307 - PAST LIFE

Have you ever had an experience that made you believe you've led a past life?

- Describe the experience and your past life

Have you ever been hypnotized and done a past life regression?

- What did you discover about your past lives?

#308 - SIXTH SENSE

Have you ever had an experience of extra sensory perception (ESP)?

- Was this experience something you sensed or something another person sensed about you?
- Did this thing actually happen?

Do you often experience ESP?

#309 - DÉJÀ VU

Déjà vu is the feeling of having experienced something before that is actually happening for the first time.

Describe a time when you experienced *déjà vu*

#310 - GYPSY

Describe a time when you had your fortune told

- Tarot cards
- Palm reading
- Crystals
- Tea leaves
- Aura reading
- Or?

Why did you decide to have your fortune told?

- Something fun to do
- Looking for guidance or answers
- You always wanted to try it
- Or?

How accurate were the predictions?

Third Love

By Ann Hamer

On the last day of my trip to Virginia I spent the afternoon wandering around Old Town Alexandria. I'd been to Staunton with my cousin to see two Shakespeare plays, to Chincoteague and Assateague to see the island ponies, and to Williamsburg and Monticello to see American history. I'd visited Shenandoah National Park to take a walk in the woods and see the views from Skyline Drive. I'd had a wonderful time, but after two weeks on the road, I was ready to go home. On that last day, before settling down for the night in my Alexandria hotel, I did what I usually do when I travel - I walked around looking at things, talked to residents and merchants, and looked for unique bookstores.

On Alexandria's historic lower King Street not too far from the Potomac River ferry landings, I chatted with a woman who offered to read my tarot cards. I don't really believe in tarot cards or fortune tellers, but I thought it would be something fun to do before I had dinner and went back to my hotel. Upstairs we went. Her place of business was musty and threadbare, and hazy from the cigarettes she smoked. The carpet was well-worn, and a dingy couch was pushed under a streaky window. In front of the couch was a chipped laminate coffee table holding the tools of her trade - a couple of decks of tarot cards, a crystal ball, and a bowl of small pebbles used for divination.

Under her direction, I shuffled the cards and divided the deck in two. She laid the cards out in a pattern meant to give a general over-view of my future. I tried to contain my usual chattiness since I know fortune tellers try to pick up hints and make it seem as though they really do know the unknown. She hinted around, looking for clues about my love life. She'd get no answers from looking at my hands since I don't wear a wedding ring. She took a stab at it.

"You will have three great loves in your life," she said in her smoker's gypsy voice.

NOOOO!! That was certainly NOT what I wanted to hear. Success with my memoir writing book and my classes - yes, certainly. Continued happiness and peace - of course. Not love. Nope. Uh-uh, absolutely not. I do not like the me I am when I am in love. I become obsessed and weird. I get depressed and moody waiting for phone calls. I put my life on hold for the current object of my affection.

I've already had two great loves in my life. The first, while I was a student at Oregon State, stepped out on me while we were living together with the woman he eventually married. The second contacted me after we had not seen each other for many years, but I had gained weight and was too ashamed to see him. He later married someone else. Besides, relationships always mean sex, and although I look pretty good when I'm fully clothed, there's nothing pretty about my naked and aging body. I'm one breast short due to cancer and a mastectomy, I have many scars from numerous surgeries, and without the snug support of Spanx, my flat rear end has the consistency of an under-baked custard. My body has gone through a lot, and while I feel strong and healthy, it shows the slings and arrows of aging and injury. It's OK for me to look at it, but I really don't want anyone else to see it unclothed.

When I got home I told Mom about the tarot card reading and my total antipathy to having another great love, since the first two didn't work out very well.

"You know," Mom said, "Great love doesn't necessarily mean romantic love."

How smart is that!!?? Mom's right of course. The love between two good friends is a great love to treasure. I feel totally open to that kind of love. And not only one more great love with one more good friend, but the love between many good friends sharing many things as we move through our lives.

I'm at peace with that and I like the idea. And believe me, none of those great loves will ever see me naked.

#311 - WHAT'S YOUR SIGN

What is your sign of the zodiac?

What are the characteristics of your sign?

- Is your personality "typical" of your sign?

Do you read your horoscope?

- Are you guided by your horoscope, or do you read it just for fun?

#312 - SUPERSTITIOUS

What are your superstitions?

#313 - SUDDEN

Write about something that changed your life suddenly and unexpectedly

- Unexpected award or honor
- Love at first sight
- Accident
- Unexpected or unanticipated move
- Unexpected death
- Unanticipated loss
- Unexpected inheritance
- A windfall
- Or?

#314 - GARDEN

How does your garden grow?

- What are you growing?
- Where does it grow?

Is this a real garden or a garden of the heart?

#315 - HAPPINESS

What experience of yours made you the happiest?

- Where do you anticipate happiness will strike next?

#316 - BUYING HAPPINESS

If you had $20,000 to buy yourself some happiness, how would you spend it?

- If you had $20,000 to buy happiness for someone else, how and on whom would you spend it?

#317 - YIN / YANG

Describe a time when you thought you were right but people said you were wrong

- About what were you right?
- What happened because you were right?

Describe a time when you thought you were right but ended up being wrong

- About what were you wrong?
- What happened because you were wrong?

#318 - SIMPLE THINGS

Sometimes it's not the big or important things that bring back memories. Sometimes it's a simple thing like the wooden spoon your mother always used to make a cake or the sweater your brother always wore when he watched a football game.

Look around your home and find a simple thing that evokes a memory

- Write about this item and your memory

HELPFUL HINT #34

REMEMBER THANKFULNESS

Cultivate the habit of being grateful for every good thing that comes to you, and to give thanks continuously. And because all things have contributed to your advancement, you should include all things in your gratitude.

- RALPH WALDO EMERSON -

Get yourself a small notebook. Write in your notebook every day at least five things for which you are thankful. These do not have to be huge things, and sometimes you may have to push yourself to find thankfulness. When this happens, try saying thanks for small things, such as "Today I am thankful I drove safely," or "Today I am thankful I have a pet." Just say thank you.

This will help you in a few ways. First, it will get you in the habit of writing. Secondly, recording your thanks may help you remember things to include in your memoir. If you write "Today I am thankful I drove safely," it may lead to memories of learning to drive, your first car, road trips, car accidents and tickets, teaching your children to drive, and other car related memories. Use your notebook to record your thanks, but also be open to its use as a tool to help you remember.

And finally, expressing gratitude will help your attitude. It will help lighten your spirit and present a more positive you to the world. And there is certainly nothing wrong with that!

#319 - THANKS

Write a thank you note to someone or something, but not a person you know

- Electronics, e.g. computer, Kindle, smart phone, TV
- A piece of furniture
- A certain food
- A holiday or other celebration
- Shoes or an article of clothing
- Car, plane, train, bike
- A favorite book or fictional character
- A favorite author or performer
- A favorite form of entertainment
- Nature, forests, ocean, mountains, plants, flowers
- One of your body parts, character traits, or physical traits
- An enjoyable sensory experience
- A certain city, state, or country
- Animals (pets or in nature)
- Modern appliances, e.g. air conditioner, refrigerator, stove, microwave
- Indoor plumbing
- Your school or education
- Your special talents or skills
- Humor and laughter
- Religious beliefs and traditions
- Freedom and liberty
- Strength and physical fitness

- Where you live
- Retirement
- Success
- Or?

This is not meant to be a list of things for which you are grateful, so try not to write things like, "I am thankful for …" Instead, write a "thank you" note to something you value. For example, if you are a book lover you might write, "Dear Kindle: Thank you for showing me a whole new world with even more books. I love you so much."

#320 - YOUR BLESSINGS

Make a list of your blessings

#321 - PLEASES

What pleases you the most about your life?

#322 - GRATITUDE

For what are you the most grateful right now?

#323 - THANKFULNESS

Describe the people in your life to whom you are grateful

- Family and friends who are a daily presence in your life
- People who did something special for you
- People who continue to do special things for you
- People who have been a long-time source of support and comfort

Life is Full of the Unexpected
by Joy Karsevar

I never thought when I moved to Upland that I would be signing up for an autobiography class. I have a senior friend who wrote her autobiography and even had it published. I thought that was great, but that was her and not me! I was happy just living life.

As I sit here today surrounded by a group of wonderful writers and women who are human, and yet so talented and brave, I cannot help but feel so grateful that I came to Upland and took the Art of Autobiography class. This class has enabled me to see myself and my life in a better light and given me the courage and skill to write my life story. I was able to deal with parts of my life story I may not have wanted to, but I am sure glad I did. My story, as with everyone's story, has to be remembered, written, revisited, relived in my mind and heart, and definitely enjoyed and passed down to loved ones and in my case, my husband Alan and children Alice and Mason, as well as my relatives, friends, and future generations of my family.

Aside from writing my story, I learned so much from my colleagues in class. Their own life stories helped me remember stories in my own life that I may have neglected or even forgotten. The stories also made me see how our lives are all interconnected. In the process a wonderful thing happened. I made new friends and got to have real down-to-earth connections with my new found friends. I got to cry with them and also laugh with them. I felt so wonderfully alive in this class.

I want to thank each one of you for your friendship, openness, and trust. I will always treasure you and our times together. I will miss you so much and I will miss our special group. But who knows, since I am kinda a gypsy and a pirate lady at heart, you may see me back in Upland or in your future travels. 'Til then … I am just an email away.

#324 - SAYING THANKS

Who are the people you wish you had thanked but didn't?

- What did these people do?

What can you do to thank these people now?

#325 - FINDING THANKS

Finding good out of bad can help change your attitude and give you a fresh perspective and a new start.

Write about a time you were able to find thankfulness in disaster or disappointment

- It could have been so much worse
- I lived through it
- I had the support and love of family and friends
- We all lived through it

- No one was too badly hurt
- We will survive
- We will rebuild

Where and how were you able to find thankfulness in a dark hour?

- How were you able to look beyond adversity to possibility?

#326 - WRITING THANKS

Write a thank you note to someone who *didn't* do something for you

- For example, in retrospect you're thankful you didn't get that job, marry that person, or take that trip

#327 - NO THANKS

Write about a time when no one thanked you

- How did you feel at the time?
- How do you feel about it now?

Write about a time when you did not say thank you

- Why didn't you say thank you?
- How can you say thank you now?

#328 - GOOD DEED

Write about a time you did a good deed

- What did you do?
- Who benefitted?

#329 - LUCK

The only time you don't find a four-leaf clover is when you stop looking for one.

- JOE RANTZ -

Are you a lucky person?

- Write about a time when you were just plain lucky

Was there a time when disaster was averted and a lucky fate seemed to intervene?

#330 - TIME CAPSULE

What item(s) would you put in a time capsule?

- Choose something representative of your life at the present time

Write a letter accompanying your item(s) to be read when the time capsule is opened in 100 years

- Describe why you selected the item(s)
- How does the item(s) represent life as it was lived?

#331 - WILD

What liberties would you like to take?

- How would you go wild?

#332 - BEST/WORST

It was the best of times, it was the worst of times ...

- CHARLES DICKENS -

What was?

#333 - YOUR DECADE

What decade is yours?

- The decade of your most vivid childhood memories
- The decade of young adulthood and your first taste of independence
- The decade in which you had your greatest financial success
- The decade in which you married or had children
- The decade in which you had your greatest triumph
- The decade in which you had your greatest disappointment or challenge
- The decade in which you overcame adversity
- The decade in which you had a major change in status

- The decade in which you had a major shift in your philosophy of life
- The decade in which you are currently living

What about your life in your decade defines you?

- How did your life in this decade influence you in later years?

What are your memories of your decade?

HELPFUL HINT #35

OLD LETTERS

Letters are among the most significant memorials a person can leave behind.

- JOHANN WOLFGANG VON GOETHE -

A few months ago I read a magazine article recommending that you get rid of clutter by throwing away old family letters. Specifically mentioned were love letters between your grandparents because after all, they are probably dead, and their letters are private, and you don't want to invade their privacy anyway.

I disagree! Old letters are a treasure. Destroying them is destroying part of your history and destroying a part of you. They tell so much more about you and your ancestors than a DNA profile. A friend of mine found a cache of love letters between her grandparents, and had them copied and bound into a book which she distributed to her family. It's such a lovely idea, and it makes a lot more sense than trashing meaningful and historic documents just so you can have a bit of extra drawer space.

Go through old letters you've saved, and use them to help you remember the things you were doing and what was important to you when they were written. If you find old letters from family members, use them to learn about your family's history. Ask your friends and family if they saved letters from you or have any family letters, and take a look at them. Quote from these old letters and weave them into the story of your life.

A word of caution though. You may come across letters that were written in anger and have a vindictive, mean, or spiteful tone. Think very hard before you use these letters, especially if the writer or the recipient are not available to explain the circumstances giving rise to the antagonistic situation.

#334 - GROWING INTO (1)

List at least ten reasons you love being over 50

- What is the best thing about growing older?

Here are some suggestions

- With maturity comes wisdom
- Less pressure and competition
- More leisure time
- Retirement
- A more relaxed frame of mind
- Self-acceptance
- Gaining a fresh perspective
- More time to spend with family and friends
- Time to try new things
- Attaining goals
- Letting go
- Or?

#335 - GROWING INTO (2)

If you are not yet over 50, list at least 10 reasons you love being your current age

#336 - CONCEPTS OF OLD AGE

What was your concept of old age when you were a child?

- How old did a person have to be to be considered "old"?

How has your idea of old age changed as you've aged?

- What age do you now consider old?

What age do you feel now?

- What age do you *think* you look?
- What age do you *really* look?

#337 - AGING BODY

What things do you like most about your body as it is today?

What things can you no longer do because of age, disability, or injury?

- Changes in stamina
- Changes in strength
- Loss of hearing
- Weakening sight
- Changing mental abilities
- And?

How do you compensate for your losses?

#338 - RETIREMENT

Whatever period of life we are in is good only to the extent that we make use of it, that we live it to the hilt, that we continue to develop and understand what it has to offer us and we have to offer it.

- ELEANOR ROOSEVELT -

How did you feel when you retired?

- Happy
- Old and useless
- Eager for new challenges
- Ready to do the things you always said you'd do if you had the time
- Looking forward to having more free time
- Lonely
- Worried about having enough money
- Or?

Did you have trouble filling your free time?

- Were you bored?

Did your retirement put any stress on your relationships?

- How did you resolve these conflicts?

Did the retirement of another person (e.g. spouse or parent) put any stress on your relationship?

- How did you resolve these conflicts?

My Louie

by Rosemary Ventura

My husband Louie always loved golf from the time he was a teenager. He caddied for golfers at Split Rock Golf Course in Pelham, New York, close to the Bronx where he lived. He became a good player himself, good enough that the golf pro at Split Rock took him under his wing and was his mentor. However, Louie's father would have none of it. He said that Louie couldn't be playing golf - "that's a game." He had to get a job and go to work. That's the way it was back then. There was no money to spend on golf lessons. He needed to bring in a salary and help the family, and he did. Louie's father was a truck driver for H.J. Korten Trucking, and he got Louie a job loading the trucks. He was 18 years old. It wasn't too long before Louie became a truck driver himself and that was the end of his golfing career until he retired and devoted most of his time to golf.

After Louie retired, he went to school to learn to be a golf instructor, and eventually taught juniors and adults how to play. Louie was a pretty good player and played in many tournaments. He loved golf so much - both teaching and playing. He even repaired golf clubs. It broke his heart and mine when, because of his back surgeries, he couldn't play anymore. He marshaled at Upland Hills Golf Course and he enjoyed that every much. He loved volunteering, first with the Upland Police Department, and then with the San Bernardino County Sheriff's Department. In spite of all the pain, he always wanted to be involved in something.

#339 - NEW PERSPECTIVES

Who or what gave you a new or fresh perspective?

- What changes did you make based on this new perspective?

#340 - CHANGING PERSPECTIVES

How have your perspectives changed as you've aged?

- About your own actions
- About the actions of others

#341 - DIFFERENT PERSPECTIVES

How have your perspectives changed as you've grown older?

- About politics
- About religion
- About your parents and family relationships
- Concepts of success
- How to be happy
- What it means to be old
- Or?

#342 - BETTER (1)

How do you make the world a better place?

- Why does it matter that you are here?

#343 - BETTER (2)

How could you have done things better?

- "I could have been a better son or daughter or mother or father or sister or brother or friend or employee or student if I had only ..."

HELPFUL HINT #36

AMBIGUITY

Some of the exercises in this book may seem unclear and ambiguous. They are designed that way. Just as you see and hear and smell things differently than others, what you read into an exercise may be different from what others read into it. Words and phrases have multiple meanings. One word spelled the same way may have two different pronunciations and two different meanings. As you write, think of different responses you can make based on different readings and different interpretations of the same word or phrase.

#344 - PRIVATE

Where do you find your privacy?

- Is having privacy important to you?

#345 - FAME

How are you famous?

- Are you well know within your area of expertise?

For what would you like to be famous?

#346 - MORE LOVE

Other than a human or an animal, what do you really love?

Tangible things, for example

- Electronics (TV, computer, tablet, smart phone, Kindle)
- Cars
- Shoes
- A country or city
- Or?

Intangible things, for example

- Music
- Art
- A certain sensory experience or sensation
- A talent or characteristic of yours
- Travel
- Or?

Concepts, for example

- Freedom
- God or your concept of a deity or higher being
- Or?

First Love

by Robert Hamer

Neither my father nor my uncle were pool players. My cousin Bruce and I were not taught how to handle the stick, about eight ball, rotation, or when to chalk the tip. We were never taken to a pool hall. It was 1936, I was twelve years old, and I wanted a pool table.

"What do you want for Christmas?" my mother asked me one dark winter afternoon as she prepared dinner.

I was sitting at the kitchen table watching her peel potatoes. "A pool table," I replied. She must have cringed.

She moved in silence from sink to refrigerator and refrigerator to stove. "That's nice," she said. "Perhaps."

From Thanksgiving to mid-December she asked repeatedly what I wanted for Christmas.

"A pool table," was my unvarying response.

In anticipation of my gift, Bruce and I spent those pre-holiday weeks making plans to spend Christmas Day shooting pool. It didn't matter that neither of us were experienced at the game. We knew we could teach each other. At the age of twelve the details of where to play, how to play, or when to play were trifles. They just didn't matter.

The Christmas tree was purchased and decorated six days before Santa's scheduled arrival, and gaily wrapped presents began to appear. First one and then a couple more, each with a card addressed to Jane or Bob or Dad or Mother. In addition to those gifts, there was always a major gift from Santa which would mysteriously appear after my sister and I had gone to bed on Christmas Eve. I was confident that sometime after bedtime, my folks would retrieve my pool table from its hiding place and install it under the tree.

Early Christmas morning my sister Jane came into my bedroom and together we went downstairs and entered the living room. We had already guessed what was in the wrapped packages, so it was the big surprise that excited us. I looked eagerly for the green felt of my pool table.

We stopped at the living room door. I was astounded to see a bike. A shiny new red and white bike with a wire basket attached to the handle bars, balloon tires, coaster brakes, and red reflectors on the rear fender.

A bike. The delight of it made me shiver. I wanted to ride it NOW!

After breakfast, Mother and Dad let me go outside to try my new bike. There were a few spills, but soon I mastered the skill of riding a two wheeler, and rode down the block to show Bruce. He had also received a red two wheeler for Christmas. My aunt greeted me from their front porch, roaring with laughter, because she had been a co-conspirator with my parents to both surprises.

I had that red bike until I enlisted in the Navy in 1944. I rode it to parks, to see girls, to the river, to music lessons - everywhere. Sometimes with Bruce, sometimes alone, but everywhere.

I loved that bike - and it was sure a lot better than a pool table.

#347 - RISKY

Do something risky and write about it.

What did you do?

- What about this activity felt risky to you?
- What does doing something risky tell you about yourself?

Does doing this risky thing give you the courage to try other risky things?

- What will you do next?

Don't compare your risky behavior to the risky behavior of others. The concept of "risk" is personal to you. Try to push yourself out of your comfort zone, but stay safe. Your goal is to challenge yourself and then write about it, not to spend time in an emergency room recovering from your risk-taking.

#348 - DANGEROUS

What is the most physically dangerous thing you have ever done?

- What made you decide to take this risk?
- How did it make you feel to take this risk?

What was the outcome?

- Were you hurt?

#349 - TIME

How are you about time?

- I'm always late
- I'm always early
- I'm always exactly on time

Was there ever a time when being late or being early had a major positive or negative impact?

- You missed an opportunity because you were too late
- You were first in line because you were early
- Or?

8

HELPFUL HINT #37

ACKNOWLEDGE, ATONE, APOLOGIZE

I have been teaching memoir writing for several years, but I'm always open to new ideas, so I recently enrolled in an autobiography writing class. During a discussion with the instructor, I mentioned two best-selling contemporary memoirs I had read and absolutely hated. I disliked the narrator of the first book because she expressed no guilt and offered no apologies for participating in the international drug trade. I disliked the narrator of the second book because she apparently found it acceptable that she and her brother first starved and then murdered their deceased mother's beloved horse. I would have liked these authors so much more if at some point they had apologized and expressed some remorse. I asked the instructor if she thought that atonement was a necessary part of memoir writing. She said perhaps not atonement, but certainly acknowledgement.

We all make mistakes and hurt others, whether intentionally or accidentally. I am not a therapist nor a spiritual advisor, and I don't know if you need to apologize to those you've hurt for the good of your soul or your mental well-being. That is an issue far beyond the scope of this book. But maybe you need to at least admit your mistakes to yourself and take personal responsibility for the unkind things you've said and done. You cannot change the past, but you can change your perception of the past, which may help you find peace, healing, and reconciliation.

Acknowledge. Atone. Apologize. Then decide what to do with it. File it away. Include it in your memoir. Give it to the person you hurt. Perform some sort of cleansing ritual.

Then treat yourself with compassion, forgive yourself for being human, and move on.

#350 - TAKE A CHANCE

Describe a time when you took a chance on someone or something

- How did it work out?

Describe a time when someone took a chance on you

- How did it work out?

#351 - DRINK

Do you drink alcohol?

- Never
- Seldom
- Only socially
- To excess

What experiences impact your decisions about drinking?

- You enjoy a social drink with friends
- You drink when you party
- You consider yourself a connoisseur
- Family history of alcohol abuse
- Observation of drunken behavior by others
- Shame or embarrassment over your own drunken behavior
- Religious convictions
- You just don't like the taste
- Or?

Describe the first time you took a drink

- A sip from an adult's drink
- Sneaking a drink after school

- At a party
- Or?

#352 - DRUNK

Describe a time when you were extremely drunk

- Do you have any regrets about how you acted?

Describe the first time you remember getting drunk

- How did you feel when you were drunk?
- How did you feel the next day?
- Were you punished the first time you got really drunk?

#353 - MEALS

What is the best meal you ever ate?

- What made it the best?

What is the worst or most disappointing meal you ever ate?

- What made it so bad?

#354 - MEMORABLE MEALS

What is the most memorable meal you've ever had?

Meals can be memorable for many reasons. This may or may not be the best food you've ever eaten

An Honest Artichoke

by Barbara Cauthorn

"Ya gotta hustle, honey," management explained, when I applied for the desperately needed job. Cocktail waitresses at Bourbon Street Jazz Jungle received no salary. Guests were encouraged to be cheerful and drink freely. Such lighthearted behavior would allow the clever cocktail waitress to earn an income.

"Don't return their change sweetie, or hold out a ten or twenty," counseled a perky fellow waitress with fluffed red hair and exquisite crimson nails. "They'll never notice. They expect it. Nobody cares. If you don't do it sweetie, you'll make zip." Being a timid person of depressing virtuousness, I was unable to apply the concept. "Oh, wait, sir," I'd call out to drunken, confused patrons, "You've forgotten your change."

So I made zip.

The good part was the music. The Jungle was celebrated for the brilliance of its New Orleans jazz bands. They were very good, almost good enough to make up for my lack of income. Bud, the lead clarinetist, was a bulky balding man with heavy jowls and deep bags under eyes that hinted of some secret depravity. He always wore the same tightly fitted Prussian blue Mafioso suit. Bud was not a handsome man, but when he picked up his clarinet and began his nightly virtuoso number, women were aware of his magnetism. Men put down their drinks. Every person in the dark, smoky room paid rapt attention when Bud swung out with "Just a Closer Walk with Thee". We listened in captivated silence as the music transformed us. A palpable layer of magic blossomed briefly in that murky room.

My boyfriend Harry and I had a ritual of after-work dinner at a local restaurant. Rizzo's, small and untouristed, was just a few doors from the Jungle. We'd find a cramped table in their tiny dimly lit back room, and sit for hours talking and feasting on stuffed artichokes and ice cold beer.

On my fourth night of unpaid Jungle servitude, Harry stopped by earlier than usual and greeted me with his breezy California grin. I knew then what must be done.

"Shall we go for artichokes?" I said.

"Sure baby, whatever you want," he said. "Right now?"

"Yes," I replied

I headed to a small room to the left of the bar where Jungle management concealed itself behind a doorway covered by a heavy compost colored curtain. The cramped space had a musty odor of cigarette butts and stale bourbon, seasoned with a splash of mildewed paper goods. The manager was a small man. He had a buzz cut, a tweedy jacket, and a dazzling, peach colored tie that might have been silk.

"I quit," I said. "Goodbye." I handed him my recently issued glossy black cocktail waitress apron with the big pockets intended to hold all the cash I wasn't making.

"No guts for it, eh?" He said. He peered at me without surprise over the top of his gold-wire rimmed glasses and caressed the apron affectionately.

Harry was waiting on the street outside. "Yeah, baby," he laughed. "Even I keep jobs longer than that. Let's eat. I'm starved."

"Me too," I said, realizing that the ache in my stomach was actually from hunger.

There are no dishonest artichokes. The good people at Rizzo's knew who we were and what we wanted. And they were marvelous. Artfully stuffed with crushed croutons, seasoned with a dash of garlic, a sprig of parsley, some fresh basil, gently caressed with a splash of extra virgin olive oil and a spatter of freshly squeezed lemon juice. Topping it all with a thick grating of parmesan, they were served steamy hot.

We sipped our frosty beers and dug deep, searching out the tender precious hearts. It was lovely. With every mouthful, I felt release from disturbing jobs and the stench of incipient debauchery. Poetry and beauty returned. Life was good.

Dawn was breaking when we walked home to Royal Street. A chill March wind was blowing in from the Gulf, heavy with salt mist and infusing the French Quarter with a restless essence that longed for the sea. We moved hurriedly, holding hands and staying out of the shadows. Only God would know who lurked in those dark, silent alleys and it wasn't the sea they were longing for.

I mused contentedly that they might benefit from a soothing dose of Rizzo's incomparable artichokes.

#355 - LIFT AND LEAN

I recently read in *Country* Magazine's Words of Wisdom, "If you can't be a lifter, don't be a leaner." I personally believe that you should know when to lean and know when to lift.

When are you and leaner and when are you a lifter?

- Are you more often a leaner or a lifter?

How do you lift others when they need to lean?

- How do others lift you when you need to lean?

#356 - ANOTHER LIFE

What other person's life would you like to lead?

- Famous person
- Family member
- Friend
- Fictional character
- Or?

Why do you want to lead this person's life?

- How is your real life like this person's life?
- How is your real life different from this person's life?

#357 - DEFAULT

What is your default setting?

#358 - TREASURED THINGS

In the book *Little Women*, the narrator Jo writes about four chests filled by sisters Meg, Amy, Beth, and Jo herself when they were children. The chests, now "Dim with dust, and worn by time," are filled with the treasured possessions of the little girls.

Find a treasure chest of your own to fill with memories. It could be a box or other container you buy or something you make. Then write about your treasures.

What did you put in your treasure chest?

- Why are these things important to you?
- What memories does each thing represent?
- Are they happy or sad memories?
- With whom did you make these memories?

Out of all the things you own, why did you choose these particular items to put into your treasure chest?

- What makes these things important in telling the story of your life?

Here are some suggestions

- Something tangible like an object or photo
- A message of love

- Something you need from another person to find healing and reconciliation
- Photos of places you love or things you like to do
- Things you like and treasure about yourself
- A future hope or a future need

These are just ideas. Fill your box with the things *you* treasure.

HELPFUL HINT #38

READ

You learn to write by writing, but you also learn to write by reading. When you read a biography, autobiography, or memoir you especially enjoy, ask yourself why you liked it. Try to incorporate some of the things you liked into your own writing.

I love to search my Kindle for out-of-print memoirs and autobiographies. I've found some treasures that I would never have found without my Kindle. These are the stories of interesting people who led fascinating lives, but are now long forgotten. Don't read just popular contemporary memoirs or the autobiographies of famous people. Look also for the stories of intriguing people whose lives are now lost to the passage of time.

#359 - DOG/CAT

What do you do in secret that only your dog or cat sees?

- What does your dog or cat know about the real you?

What type of a person does your dog or cat think you are?

#360 - ANIMALS

Write about your memory of an animal

- Your first pet
- Your favorite pet
- An animal that scared you
- A friend's pet
- A sighting or encounter with a wild animal

- A fictional animal you may have cried over or wished you owned
- A type of animal that you just don't like

What do you like about animals?

- What do you dislike about animals?

#361 - LIKING ANIMALS

Sometimes I like animals more than

- Friends
- Relatives
- Spouse
- Co-workers
- People in general
- Or?

Why?

#362 - FEARING ANIMALS

Do you fear any animals?

- An individual animal
- A particular breed, e.g. pit bulls
- A particular species, e.g. all cats
- Wild animals

Why do you fear these animals?

- A bad experience
- Something you read or heard
- Or?

#363 - YOUR TYPE OF ANIMAL

Are you a "dog person" or a "cat person"?

- Why?

#364 - PETS

Describe your family pets

- As a child
- As an adult
- Now

Did you have one pet that was extra special to you?

- Why was this pet more special than the others?

Do you have a pet no longer with you that you still miss?

Taffy

by Sallie Ringle

It was Christmas Eve 1953, and the family was sitting at the dining table. I heard jingle bells. The bells were really loud and right outside our house. There was a "Ho Ho Ho" and a knock at the door. Mom asked me to answer it. I opened the door and there was Santa. Tucked under his arm was a little brown and white puppy with floppy ears and a huge red bow. There was a tag on the bow and it read "Sallie & Steve". My brother Steve came running up and so did my cousins. We all crowded around Santa. He asked if we thought we were old enough to take care of a puppy. Of course we said YES! That night reinstated my belief in Santa Claus. At nine I thought I was too big to believe in him. I was wrong. Santa had come and brought me a puppy. He brought her on Christmas Eve because he was afraid that riding in his sleigh would be too hard for a little puppy and she might get cold.

Being the older sister, I latched on to the dog first. She was so soft and kissed me right away all over my face. Dad had made a place where we were to keep the puppy until she was housebroken. Mom said we needed to give her a name. Everyone had an idea. Mom suggested we call her Taffy because her coat was the color of salt water taffy with white. So we agreed - Taffy it would be.

Taffy became my confidant over the years. I taught her to walk and heel, first on a leash, but in time she was so good walking I could take her on long walks without the leash and she would never leave my side. She would always come bounding home when we called or Dad whistled for her. As I got to be 12 to 14 years old I would take Taffy on walks to secluded places and talk to her. Sometimes I would cry because I was an emotional teen and needed someone to talk to. Taffy was the best friend I had. I continued to pay lots of attention to my beloved dog Taffy, even in my high school years.

I have had many dogs over the years but Taffy was always my favorite. She was my best friend when I needed one. I left home when I was 18 and my brother left a couple of years after that. Mom and Dad decided to sell the family home and move into a condo. Steve was off at college, I had moved to northern California, and Mom and Dad decided they didn't want to take Taffy to live in the condo. They never consulted my brother or me. They just took her to the animal shelter to be adopted. Who would adopt a 12 year old dog? I have always been sure that the shelter put her down. For years I resented my parents for doing that to Taffy. She deserved to be loved to the end. I will always love her.

#365 - DIFFERENT

In what ways are you different from other people?

- Do you embrace your differences or would you rather be like everyone else?

#366 - DROP THE REINS

He acquired the use of a discarded donkey, saying, as he let the reins fall and gave the beast its head, settling himself on its back, and taking out a pencil and a manuscript book: "Go where thou wilt my friend. I confine myself to thy taste and good behavior."

- ELEANOR CALHOUN -

Where is your donkey taking you?

- Is this a real or an imaginary place?
- Where are you when you mount up?
- Is this a physical destination or a state of mind?
- Is this destination in the past, the present, or the future?

Is it difficult for you to trust your donkey?

- Is your imaginary donkey more headstrong than you expected?

As you do this exercise, use your imagination and try not to let your writing be limited by logic. Think freely and let your donkey fly through space and time. Just start writing and have some fun.

#367 - GIFTS

What is the best gift you ever received?

- Holiday gift
- Birthday gift
- Wedding gift
- Unexpected gift
- Or?

What is the gift you always wanted but never received?

- The puppy or pony you wanted as a child
- Your first car
- A special Valentine's Day gift
- An engagement ring
- Or?

As a child, what practical gifts did you always receive for holidays and birthdays?

- Socks and underwear
- Tooth brush and tooth paste
- Stamps
- School supplies
- Clothes
- Or?

What gift were you given that you would willingly "re-gift" or donate to charity because it was absolutely wrong for you?

- How did it make you feel to be given the "wrong" gift, especially if the gift was from someone you thought knew you well?

#368 - GIVING GIFTS

What is the best gift you ever gave?

What gift did you give that fell absolutely flat?

#369 - BUYING GIFTS

What do you think about when you shop for gifts?

- Love
- Obligation
- Resentment
- Memories
- Happiness
- And?

What gifts do you make rather than buy?

- Baked goods
- Hand crafts and art pieces
- Personal messages and poems
- Or?

#370 - GIFTS OF LOVE

On the first day of Christmas, my true love gave to me a partridge in a pear tree.

- TRADITIONAL -

Describe a gift you received from your true love

- What were your feelings when you received this gift?

Describe a gift you gave to your true love

- What were your feelings when you gave this gift?
- How did your true love react to receiving this gift?

HELPFUL HINT #39

LET YOUR VOICE BE HEARD

Do you ever long to hear again the voice of someone you loved who is now lost to you?

The sound of your voice is unique, and you can leave the gift of your voice as part of your legacy. Choose a few of your stories, and then record yourself telling these stories. This recording will make a treasured addition to your written memoir.

#371 - INTELLIGENCE

What kind of intelligence do you have?

- Book learning
- Emotional intelligence
- Intuitive intelligence
- Empathy or sympathy
- Creative intelligence
- "Street smarts"
- Good sense
- Or?

What kind of intelligence do you lack?

- What kind of intelligence do you wish you had?

#372 - TIP

What is the best tip you ever received?

- For service, e.g. serving food in a restaurant
- An investment or employment opportunity
- A place to visit
- An educational opportunity
- Or?

What are you willing to do for a good tip?

#373 - SETTING GOALS

What do you hope to do and to accomplish in your lifetime?

- In your 20s?
- In your 30s?
- In your 40s?
- In your 50s?
- In your 60s?
- In your 70s?
- In old age?

#374 - BUTTONS

What is the fastest way to make you angry?

- What are your "hot buttons"?

#375 - JUDGMENT

I judge people on two things - do they tip and do they love dogs.

- ROBERT WUHL -

On what do you judge people?

HELPFUL HINT #40

IT'S NOT ALL ABOUT YOU

Beware of using too much "I, I, I" and "me, me, me". While it's true that this is the story of your life, you don't live in a bubble. You meet other people and are impacted by them. If you are not honest about the role others play in your life and it is too much "I, I, I" and "me, me, me", then you are not telling your complete story.

To avoid too much self-absorption, every so often practice writing as an observer.

- Write about something you've seen, but not your reaction to seeing it
- Put yourself in another person's place, and write from that person's perspective

- Describe an unfamiliar place without describing how you felt being there

---

#376 - RICHES

What are "riches" to you?

- Family
- Friends
- Money
- Career
- Spirit
- Faith
- New experiences
- Travel
- Or?

In what ways are you rich?

#377 - JEALOUSY

What makes you jealous?

- People with nicer homes, cars, or other possessions
- People with more money
- People with professional success
- People with personality characteristics you admire
- People you consider more attractive or smarter than you
- People with lots of friends
- People with loving spouses and successful children
- Or?

How do you act when you feel jealous?

- How can you overcome your feelings of jealousy?

#378 - ATTACK

Have you ever been attacked?

Describe the attack

- A physical attack such as an assault
- An attack on your character or integrity
- An attack by someone you trusted such as a relative, co-worker, or friend

How did you react to being attacked?

- Do you have any vivid memories or flashbacks as a result of this attack?

How was the issue resolved?

- Arrest of the attacker
- Confrontation with the attacker
- Apology from the attacker
- There was no resolution
- Or?

#379 - VULNERABLE

When do you feel vulnerable?

- Physically
- Spiritually
- Emotionally

How do you deal with your vulnerability?

#380 - CRIME

Have you ever been the victim of a crime?

- What happened to you?

Was the criminal prosecuted?

- Did you testify in court?
- Was the criminal convicted?

Do you have any long term physical or emotional problems as a result of this crime?

The Intruder

by Lynda Barr

It saddens me to realize that it sometimes takes the threat of losing your child to remind you just how precious their life is to you. In January 1989, my 17 year old son Jeff had just started living with his dad in Chino, and my 15 year old daughter Robin was living with me. While I was working the 3:00 p.m. to 11:00 p.m. shift at IOLAB Corporation in Claremont, I received a very sobering call from an Upland police officer. He told me that my house had been broken into and my daughter was OK but very upset. He wanted me to come home as soon as I could. I immediately felt panicky, but tried to keep myself calm so I could drive the four miles home without getting a speeding ticket or into an accident.

When I came into my house, several policemen and a large German shepherd dog were there. One of the policemen was questioning my daughter who was shaking uncontrollably and crying. Robin's next words were, "He then came into my bedroom and sat down on my back with a leg on each side of me and that's when I started screaming." When I heard her words my mouth fell open and visions of my mother-in-law being murdered by the Night Stalker just three years earlier painfully entered my mind!

I knew full well that I could have lost my child if the intruder had the same malicious intentions as my mother-in-law's intruder had. Suddenly I welcomed my daughter's crying and shaking. It was living proof that she was still very much alive. I vowed then that no other person would again violate the privacy of our home or terrorize my daughter! With money that my work lent me, I secured the house with new locks, security lights, and a peek hole in the front door.

Robin and I became a lot closer and much more concerned about each other's safety and welfare, especially when we knew that one of us would be home alone. I thanked God everyday that I still had a daughter I could love, hug, and share my life with. Robin, who is now 43, and her husband Mike now have two daughters of their own. And life continues on ...

#381 - CRIMINAL

Have you ever broken the law?

- What was your crime?

What was the aftermath of your crime?

- You got away with it
- You were arrested
- You were fined
- You were tried and convicted
- You were placed on probation
- You went to jail

#382 - LIAR LIAR

What was the biggest lie you ever told?

- What happened as the result of this lie?

#383 - MANIPULATION

Are you manipulated or a manipulator?

- How do you manipulate?
- How are you manipulated?

#384 - REPENT

If I repent of anything, it is very likely to be my good behavior.

- HENRY DAVID THOREAU -

About what do you repent?

#385 - CALL BACK

How did your failure to return a call or answer a letter or email change your life?

- Was the change positive or negative?

What happened?

#386 - DID IT

I didn't think I could do it, but I did

- What did you do?
- Why did you think you couldn't do it?

HELPFUL HINT #41
EXPLAIN YOURSELF

In an ancient Buddhist story, a group of blind men is asked to describe an elephant by feeling different parts of its body. One man feels the leg and says the elephant looks like a pillar. One man feels the tail and says the elephant looks like a rope. And one man feels the tusk and says the elephant looks like a pipe.

Like the men in the story, we look at things from our own perspective, making it easy to misjudge the actions and motivations of others. Do not assume people understand your reasons for the actions you've taken and the decisions you've made.

Explain yourself. Tell your readers who you are. Let your words paint the picture you want your readers to have of you. You do not want others to have false ideas about you based on their own perspectives, misconceptions, or misunderstandings.

#387 - SHOULDN'T (1)

Describe something you were told not to do, but did anyway

- What was the result of your doing this thing?
- Were you glad you did this thing, or did you later regret it?

Describe something you wish you had been told not to do

- Why do you regret doing this thing?
- Would you have listened if someone had told you not to do it?

#388 - SHOULDN'T (2)

Describe something your "inner voice" told you not to do but you went ahead and did anyway

- What was the result of your doing this thing?
- Were you glad you did it, or did you later have regrets?

#389 - BETTER THAN

"There is nothing better than ..."

- There nothing better than what in your world?

#390 - PARK

Describe your favorite park

- National park or forest
- Neighborhood park
- Amusement park
- City park
- Vacant lot
- Wild or undeveloped area

Describe a special memory of this park

#391 - SPORTING LIFE

What is your favorite sport?

- To play?
- To watch?

Describe a special memory of either playing or watching this sport

#392 - WINNING

Describe a time when you won a prize

- What did you do to win this prize?

Describe the prize you won

Athletic Prowess

by Robert Hamer

In 1956 golf was not a serious recreational pursuit. My own clubs came third hand from my father who got them second hand from my uncle. I played infrequently on public courses and never took lessons. My skill level never rose above inept.

My employer belonged to a business association which held a fun-fest once a year with golf in the morning, late afternoon gin rummy and cocktails, and concluded with dinner and an awards presentation. My boss made it clear that participation was part of my job description.

On a warm spring morning, thirty foursomes teed-off at Riviera Country Club. My own shot left the first tee straight and true, but then ever so gently started to curve right, finally hitting the ground after making a complete right turn. The short shots were not much better, but enough of an improvement to be less hazardous to others in the foursome, on the course, and all wildlife in general. My strokes per hole ranged from eight to ten, and only the par threes saved me from high single and low double digits on every hole.

The tee for the eighteenth fairway at Riviera is at the bottom of a modestly steep hill. The green and cup are at the top of the hill, and neither is visible from the tee. A twenty foot tall periscope allows a golfer on the eighteenth tee to see if the preceding foursome has cleared the green. I was the last in our foursome to tee-off. My ball hit the side of the hill and rolled back down a third of the way. My second shot hit further up the hill and again rolled back. Finally the hill was ascended, the green achieved, and the hole and round completed.

That evening trophies were awarded to players for low net, low gross, and to the winner. My name was called to receive the award for high gross. I opened the booby prize in front of the cat-calling and abusive audience.

I had shot 151.

#393 - ACCOMPLISHMENT

Other people may find this easy, but it wasn't for me, and when I did it, it was a real accomplishment and I was proud

- Describe what you did

How did this accomplishment make you feel?

Here are some suggestions

- Cooked a gourmet meal
- Baked a cake
- Fixed a computer problem
- Took a solo trip
- Chaired a committee
- Spoke in public
- Rode a horse
- Swam in the ocean
- Took a hike
- Asked for a raise
- Sang in public
- Stood up to a bully
- Earned a paycheck
- Beat all levels of a video game
- Or?

#394 - IMPORTANT THINGS

What are the ten most important things in your life?

- Most important things as a child
- Most important things as a teenager
- Most important things as a young adult
- Most important things now

What about these things makes them important to you?

#395 - THOUGHT

What is your food for thought?

#396 - PROUD

What is your proudest accomplishment?

- Family and children
- Career or profession
- Achievements in education or sports
- Winning an election or award
- Conquering a personal challenge, e.g. acquiring patience or overcoming shyness
- Mending broken relationships
- Overcoming illness or injury
- A time you behaved kindly or honorably
- A time you were brave
- Overcoming adversity or bad news
- Being happy and contented
- Or?

#397 - NECESSARY

It is no use saying, "We are doing our best." You have got to succeed in doing what is necessary.

- WINSTON CHURCHILL -

When did you succeed in doing what was necessary?

- What did you do?

#398 - ORPHAN

No matter how old you are, after your parents die you may feel like an orphan.

How did you feel when you were first orphaned?

- How old were you when you were orphaned?

How do you now feel about being an orphan?

- Do you still miss your parent(s)?

Describe how you felt after one parent had died, but you still had a surviving parent

- How did that feeling differ from the way you felt after both of your parents had died?

Do you sometimes feel like an orphan even though your parents are alive?

- Why do you feel like an orphan?
- Have your feelings led to an estrangement from your parents or family?
- Can the estrangement be healed?

Are you now a caretaker for one or both of your parents?

- Does this role reversal make you feel orphaned?

9

HELPFUL HINT #42

GO TO THE SOURCE

We have a tendency to believe that things are true simply because they are written down. You don't want a falsehood or misunderstanding to become accepted as true just because you put it down on paper.

Use primary sources to verify information. Don't write that your sister was motivated to do something based on guesswork and your own biased observation if you are able to talk with her and hear her version of the story. If you need to verify facts with older friends and relatives, talk with them before it is too late and they are no longer available due to death or disability.

#399 - ADVICE

What is the best piece of advice you've been given?

What is the best piece of advice you gave to someone else?

#400 - HEALTH

What diseases, illnesses, or accidents have happened as you've matured and aged?

- What are your current health issues?

Describe any illness, injury, or chronic conditions that have changed your life

- Physical or mental limitations
- Inability to engage in activities due to health issues
- Changes to long and short term plans
- Fear
- Or?

#401 - ILLNESS

How do you respond to illness?

- To your own illness
- To the illness of family members or friends

Are you a good patient?

- Do you like being cared for or would you rather be left alone?

How well do you tolerate the discomfort of treatment?

- Do you do follow your doctor's advice, or know what's best for you and act accordingly?

#402 - STRONG

How are you strong?

- Physically strong
- Mentally strong
- Emotionally strong
- Spiritually strong

#403 - TREATMENT

If you or a loved one has ever been in long-term medical treatment, you know that over time it can be many things: draining or exhausting, ridiculous, tragic, frustrating, frightening, and sometimes even funny.

Write about a situation when you or a loved one was hospitalized or in long-term medical treatment

- What led to the hospitalization or long-term treatment?
- Impacts of this long-term hospitalization or treatment on the patient, on you, and on other family members
- Impacts of any continuing disability or medical needs after the hospitalization or treatment ended

HELPFUL HINT #43

DEVELOPING CHARACTER

Your memoir is about real events that happened to real people, but you can still use fiction writing techniques to develop character. Make your characters come alive by asking:

- What is this person hiding or hiding from?
- What is this person absolutely in love with or consumed by?
- What is this person's passion?
- What keeps this person awake at night?

You will be more real to your readers if you also answer the same questions when writing about yourself.

#404 - WALKING

Go take a walk, and then write about your thoughts

#405 - GUILTY

About what do you feel guilty?

#406 - ANGER

What stresses or angers you?

- Is what stresses or angers you now different from what stressed or angered you when you were younger?

How do you deal with your stress and anger?

#407 - NEW REALITY

Things may happen suddenly or unexpectedly that change your reality. You go from being a spouse to being widowed. You go from being healthy and fit to a person with physical challenges. You go from employed to unemployed, or financially secure to insolvent.

What happened to you or your family that led to a new reality?

- How did you cope with it?
- How did your family cope with it?
- What changes did your new reality cause you to make?

Have things improved for you?

#408 - LIFE LESSON

What life lesson or profound truth did you learn from a serious or life threatening illness or injury?

- Strength
- Perseverance
- How much you are loved and supported by others
- Ability to deal with profound loss
- Strength of character
- Assertiveness
- Or?

Accidents and Epiphanies
by Ann Hamer

A few weeks ago my friend Joan gave me Stephen King's *On Writing* for my birthday. At the end of the book, King writes about being hit by a car while out taking a walk. Since I was also hit by a car while out taking a walk, I wanted to write to him and say, "Me too, me too," but I'm sure there were lots of people who wrote him to say, "Me too," so I didn't. Here's what I wanted to say.

Stephen King's leg was shattered and his hip broken. I broke both my legs, both my arms, my ankle, my shoulder, and my collarbone. He had multiple surgeries to repair his leg. I had one surgery to rebuild my shoulder and put pins in my ankle. He went home from the hospital and began walking three weeks after his accident. I spent 2½ months in the hospital and four months in a wheelchair before I started walking again. It took us both lots of very painful rehab and hard work to get to where we are today. I can't speak for Stephen King, but I know for myself that today I am pretty good. There are things I will never do again - ride a bike, swim in the ocean, walk on sand or on an uneven or rocky surface. I can't run, and it is difficult for me to lift my left arm over my head. But I am strong and happy and I can walk and talk and read and think and write and teach my classes, and for that I am very grateful.

When people hear about my accident they always ask if the man who ran me over was texting. He was 72 years old, so I don't think so. He was turning left. I was in a crosswalk with a green light and a walk signal, and he just didn't see me. He told the police he didn't see me until I hit his windshield.

Yes, he stopped. I don't remember actually getting hit, but once I was on the ground I was conscious and aware of everything. I saw him. He was standing with a woman who saw him hit me. She had stopped and called 911. She was a nurse and spoke to me. She was so kind. The man who ran me over never said a word to me. Wouldn't you think that if you'd run over someone you'd say something like, "Ohmygod are you all right??" Nope. Not him.

No, I didn't sue him. The attorney I hired did an asset search, but he had multiple prior judgments and two tax liens, so there was no point. I guess if you're going to get hit by a car, you should try to see to it that the car is driven by Bill Gates' chauffeur and not a tax-evading scofflaw.

I think Stephen King and I can agree on a few points:

1. In a car vs. pedestrian encounter, the car will win.
2. It hurts a lot to get hit by a car.
3. All in all, NOT being hit by a car is a whole lot better than being hit by a car.

Since I am approaching the fourth anniversary of being run over, I've been thinking a lot about the accident. Mostly I've been thinking about my big take-aways. My biggest take-away was that when it came right down to it, I really had only two choices. I could lie in bed, become an invalid, and wait to die, or I could get up and do the best I could do every day. I could be resilient. That's what I did back then, and that's what I still try to do today. Sometimes my best is really good, sometimes it's OK, and sometimes it's not much better than, "Well at least today I got dressed." Like everyone, there are days when I'm depressed or crabby or lazy. But mostly I try to do the best that I can do every day. I think that's pretty much everyone's choice. Do the best you can do, because your only other choice is to just give up.

Everyone's life is full of challenges. You never know how your life will change, but change it will, and sometimes those changes happen overnight. Sometimes the change is good - sudden love or an unexpected promotion. Sometimes the change is challenging - death, illness, injury, abandonment. You may be fortunate and have the help, love, and support of family and friends (as I did in great abundance), but in the end it's up to you to get up every day and do the best that you can do. I hope Stephen King agrees.

#409 - PROTECTION

How do you protect yourself?

- Who else protects you?

#410 - HALF-GLASS

Is your glass half-empty or half-full?

#411 - MUSIC

*Sometimes it's the artist's task to find out
how much music you can make with what you have left.*

- ITZHAK PERLMAN -

How much music do you have left?

- What is the sound of your music?
- How do you express your music?

Will you express your music with an instrument, your voice, or is it metaphorical music that you hold in your heart?

#412 - RESOLUTION

It doesn't need to be New Year's Eve for you to make a resolution

- Make one

What will you do to accomplish your resolution?

- Do you think you'll be able to do it?

#413 - TRAILS

Do not go where the path may lead; go instead where there is no path and leave a trail.

- RALPH WALDO EMERSON -

What is the trail you are leaving?

- Where is your trail leading you?

Who or what walks the trail with you?

HELPFUL HINT #44

USE A DISGUISE

There may be times when you want to protect the privacy or identity of another person. You can do this by creating a disguise. Use false names or change the date or location of the event you are describing.

#414 - ARRIVED

Where do you go when you go there?

- In your Mind
- In your Body
- In your Spirit

#415 - LIGHTER

Do you have a light heart?

- How is your heart light?

If your heart is heavy, what can you do to make it lighter?

- Is your heart lighter now than when you were younger?

#416 - WITH

Whom do you wish was with you now?

#417 - FEAST

Ernest Hemingway once described life as a "moveable feast".

Is your life a moveable feast or something a bit less tasty?

#418 - FEAR

When were you really afraid?

- Describe a time when you felt unsafe or vulnerable

How do you protect yourself?

- Pepper spray
- A gun or knife
- Security measures in your home
- Taking martial arts or self-protection classes
- Your invincible attitude
- Or?

Fear - A Roller Coaster Ride of Emotions

by Lynda Barr

I was divorced from my first husband Dale for eight years by July 1985, and we had the rhythm down on which weekends our son and daughter would be staying with him and his wife Vivian, and who would do the picking up and dropping off for each visit. My son Jeff had just turned 14 and his sister Robin was 12.

It was my turn to pick up the kids from Dale's home on Sunday, July 7th, and I came up to his front door and knocked. Dale answered but didn't say a word and looked very much in shock. I didn't see or hear the kids, and noticed Dale's brother and his wife were there and looked like they had been crying. Very quickly my fear mounted, and I could feel my adrenalin pumping since I assumed something had happened to one or both of my kids. I immediately imagined them killed in some horrible accident and that it must have just happened. I could barely breathe and felt very panicky and demanded that he tell me what happened. He said, "My mom was murdered by the Night Stalker."

To this day I still feel so much guilt in the split-second of immediate relief I felt that my kids were alive. Then, in the next few seconds my emotions returned to a horrified feeling. As I entered his home, I asked Dale how he knew it was the Night Stalker who killed his mom. He told me the police had come and let him know she had been murdered that morning at 2:30 a.m., and gave him the reasons why they knew it was Richard Ramirez. My kids came out from one of the other rooms, and I saw they were very upset and crying. I tried to console them, but knew nothing would ever bring back their only living Grandma.

The next few weeks continued to be extremely tense since the Night Stalker was still on the loose and still killing. When Richard Ramirez saw his photo in the newspapers on August 31, 1985, he panicked and began running through an east LA neighborhood. Within minutes, he was recognized and caught by angry residents, and was being kicked and beaten with a tire iron. Unfortunately the police arrived too soon and he was arrested and taken away.

Richard Ramirez, who was then 25 years old, had begun terrorizing southern California in late 1984. He murdered thirteen people and brutalized two dozen more during the next year. Three years later his trial began, and Dale and other family members attended as many of the court proceedings as they could. What made the horror of those days continue for surviving victims and their families was the way Richard Ramirez was so callously arrogant during the court proceedings, and how he laughed as the details of each murder were read in court. He was eventually convicted of first degree murder in all cases plus thirty more felonies, and sentenced to death.

Richard Ramirez died at Marin General Hospital in Greenbrae, California on June 7, 2007 at the age of 53. He died from complications related to B-cell lymphoma while awaiting execution on California's Death Row at San Quentin. News of his death traveled fast, and finally gave some long awaited closure to many people. The date of his death was one day after my son Jeff's 35th birthday, and was probably his best gift that year.

#419 - FEARFUL

What did you not do because you were afraid?

Why were you afraid?

- Health issues
- Money issues
- Lack of confidence in your abilities
- Unwilling to take a risk
- Fear of physical harm
- Phobias, e.g. fear of heights or speaking in public
- Feelings of danger or threat
- Or?

Were you able to overcome your fear?

- Did you learn any lessons from your inaction due to fear that changed the way you lead your life?

#420 - CONQUERING FEAR

What fear do you have that you want to conquer?

- How do you plan to conquer this fear?

#421 - GUARDIAN

Describe your Guardian Angel

- Female, male, nonsexual being
- Human or non-human form
- Wings?

How do you experience the presence of this angel in your life?

- Do you see your guardian angel?
- Does your guardian angel appear in your dreams?
- Does your guardian angel perform miracles in your life?

Do you pray to your guardian angel?

#422 - MIRACLES

Where do you find miracles in your life?

- Do miracles just seem to happen to you?
- Do you find miracles when you actually look for them?

How are you able to find miracles in life's small things?

#423 - RISE

How did you rise to the occasion?

- What happened?
- What did you do?

HELPFUL HINT #45

JOURNALS ARE NOT MEMOIRS

If you have kept journals throughout your life, you may think that all you have to do to create your memoir is transcribe your journals onto your computer. Journals are not memoirs. Journals can be introspective, critical, and sometimes even bitchy and self-absorbed. You want your readers to be interested in your life, and not think of you as a whiny cry-baby. Too much introspection is boring and will never tell your readers the whole story.

Use your journals to remember where you were, what you were doing, and how you felt at certain times of your life. You may be tempted to use your journals to re-examine your mental state, but try to find a place other than your memoir for psychological musings. You can put them in your second book!

#424 - PRECIOUS

In what way is your life precious to you?

- If your life does not feel precious right now, how can you make it precious to you in the future?

#425 - FREE DAY

What would you do on a day with no obligations, no appointments, and absolutely nothing you had to do?

#426 - WORRY

Are you a worrier?

- What things do you worry about?

#427 - THREAT

Write about a time when you felt threatened

#428 - WAR

Wars and revolutions go down in history in one light.
Those who actually experience them see them in another.

- LILIE DE FERNANDEZ-AZABAL -

Your memories and thoughts of war are truly of your time and place. My mother's memories are of the "good" war, World War II, and her work in an aircraft factory assembling planes for combat. My memories are of a different time and a different war. I remember my brothers playing "war" games when we were kids, but my own memories of war are of Vietnam and anti-war protests. You may have memories of combat, the return from war of a parent you had not seen for years, or family stories and memories of incarceration in internment or concentration camps or living in occupied territory. If you have no memories of war, feel blessed that you have lived in peace, and move on to the next topic.

Which war is "your" war?

Write about your war memories

- Military service
- Branch and rank
- Combat

- Military support services
- Anti-war protester

Did you earn any medals or commendations?

- Describe the action for which you earned your citation

Were you injured?

- Describe how you were injured

What memories do you have of your "comrades in arms?"

What impact did your military service have on your later life?

- Benefits provided under the GI Bill
- Where you chose to live after your service
- Post-war career choices
- A change in your basic attitudes and philosophy of life
- On-going effects from a wound or post-traumatic stress
- Or?

What was it like to return to civilian life?

How did the military service of a family member impact your own life?

How Our Family Survived the War

by Joy Karsevar

told in the voice of her father Ricardo Tomacruz

I was barely 17 when World War II broke out in the Philippines. We heard news of the Japanese attack on Pearl Harbor over the radio. Due to the time difference, we heard on Monday morning, and I was in school. We were having a flag ceremony. I remember there were two flags - the Philippine flag and the American flag. The Philippines was then a Commonwealth of the United States. An announcement came from the school authorities, "NO SCHOOL!" We all cheered! "HOORAY!!" Little did we realize it would be the last time we would be in high school, and there would be no more school for four years.

Life changed instantly. The Japanese bombed Manila. There was death, chaos, and evacuations everywhere. The Japanese put up sentry posts where we had to line up, bow to them, and get checked. I can still hear them shouting, KORA, KORA, KORA!" meaning, "LIS-

TEN!" They would slap anyone who did not fall in line or bow to them. Our once upper class lifestyle changed overnight. It was war time. Our cars and properties were confiscated. We were down to only being able to put food on the table and stay alive.

When the Japanese bombed our city on Christmas Day, our family decided it was time to evacuate. We moved south to Hagonoy province, and later to Manila. There were more killings and torture at the whim of the Japanese army. Our house in Cabanatuan was occupied by Japanese nurses without our knowledge or permission. They made it their home for the duration of the war.

My father converted our wagon-car into a pick-up van to avoid ambushes. It ran on alcohol since there was no gasoline. We had to apply for alcohol, and there was a ration of 100 liters for three months. A hundred liters was good for only one round trip from Manila to Cabanatuan, and we needed to transport rice. My 19 year old brother Louie would apply for alcohol and show a business card he had from a pre-war Japanese friend of my dad who was a Colonel in the Japanese army. Before the war the Colonel and my dad did business, and he became a good friend. His card helped us get a double ration of alcohol, and again later in a way we never could have imagined.

In the last six months of the war, my family decided to go back to our province because we had no more food in Manila. Things were all right for a while, although a lot of the locals told us not to stay since there were fierce Japanese soldiers in the area, but we did not listen. We were just too lax.

One day my mom and Louie were hanging white sheets outside on the laundry line. The Japanese saw this and thought they were giving signals to the American fighter planes. They came to our house and arrested my dad and my brother, and accused them of helping the Americans. My mom, the rest of my siblings, and I were not arrested, and to this day I do not know why.

They brought my dad to a field and were ready to kill him, when luckily he remembered the business card of his Japanese Colonel friend. His friend had said, "Show my card when it is a matter of life and death." He showed it to his Japanese captors, and they were impressed my dad knew the Colonel since he was a respected and high ranking officer. They drove my brother Louie far away from us, and we really thought they would kill him. We were so sad and thought we would never see him again. We were shocked to see him walking home 24 hours later. We asked what made them release him. He said that when he was in the vehicle he started talking with a Japanese officer who spoke good English, and was so impressed with Louie that he felt compassion and released him.

We felt so happy. We were ecstatic when the next day the Japanese surrendered and the war was over. Our family of ten was so blessed not to have had a single prisoner or casualty of war.

#429 - SURVIVOR

Do you have any survivor guilt?

- You survived when others didn't
- Your injuries were less severe than those of other survivors

How did you deal with your survivor guilt?

- Learned to accept it
- Felt gratitude for your survival
- Tried to forget what happened
- Tried to convince yourself that things were a lot worse for you than they actually were in order to feel something in common with others
- Or?

#430 - ELECTED

Describe a time when you won an election

- Who were your competitors?
- What was your campaign strategy?

What did you accomplish while in office?

#431 - ALSO RAN

Describe a time when you didn't win, came in last or were an "also ran"

- Did you try a second time, or was once enough?
- If you tried a second time, what was the result?

#432 - ELECTIONS

Politics is the participation of the citizen in his government.
The kind of government he has depends entirely on the quality of that participation.

- ELEANOR ROOSEVELT -

Describe the first national or presidential election in which you voted

- For whom did you vote?
- Why?
- Did you work on the campaign?

How have your politics changed as you've aged?

#433 - ACTIVISM

A foolish faith in authority is the worst enemy of truth.

- ALBERT EINSTEIN -

Have you ever been an activist?

What issues are important to you?

- Politics
- Peace and anti-war issues
- Gun control
- Women, racial, LGBTQ rights
- Labor issues and workers' rights
- Religious issues
- Environmental issues
- Healthcare
- Crime
- Consumer protection

- Government corruption
- Or?

Describe your activism

- Campaigning for candidates
- Writing letters and petitioning political leaders
- Marches
- Rallies
- Grass roots campaigning
- Public speaking
- Fundraising
- Donating money
- Blogging or posting comments online
- Or?

HELPFUL HINT #46

KEEP A JOURNAL ANYWAY

While it's true that a journal is not a memoir, keep a journal anyway. It will get you in the habit of writing, and when you re-read your journal in years to come, you will be amazed at the depth of your own wisdom. Re-reading your journal can help you think about your life, your actions, and the actions of others.

#434 - ACCIDENTAL

Michael Kimmelman wrote a book titled *The Accidental Masterpiece: On the Art of Life and Vice Versa*.

What is your accidental masterpiece?

#435 - FEATHER AND FUR

If you could be any animal, what animal would you be?

- Would you choose to be a wild animal, a domesticated animal, a bird, a reptile, or your own well-loved pet?

Why do you want to be this animal?

- How would you act if you were this animal?

#436 - DRESS UP

What costume would you wear to a costume party?

- Funniest costume
- Sexiest costume
- Scariest costume
- Most inventive costume
- Or?

Was this costume homemade, rented, or store bought?

- If homemade, who made the costume for you?

Have you ever worn this costume, or is it your fantasy costume?

- If you have worn this costume, how did it make you feel?
- How did other people react to you? Did you like their reactions?

If you have never worn this costume, why not?

#437 - MASK

What is the mask you wear?

#438 - SECRETS (1)

Describe a time when you told someone else's secret

- Why did you tell this person's secret?

What happened as a result of your telling this secret?

- Loss of friendship
- People considered you untrustworthy
- The person whose secret you told was punished in some way
- Or?

#439 - SECRETS (2)

Describe a time when someone told your secret

- Why did this person tell your secret?

What was the result?

- Loss of friendship
- That person was considered untrustworthy by you and others
- You were punished in some way
- Or?

#440 - SECRETS (3)

Describe a time when you told a secret of your own

- Why did you choose to tell your secret?
- What was the result?

HELPFUL HINT #47

USE DIALOG

Weave conversations into your story. In the example below, notice how the character and personality of the narrator is established with just a few lines of dialog.

Teeth

by Robert Hamer

As a child, my twice a year visits to the dentist were as regular as the equinox. After one visit, the dentist handed me a package of Wrigley's Juicy Fruit gum and said, "Chew lots of this."

He may have included admonitions about time, place, and frequency, but these were all lost on me. So chew I did. From the end of my dental appointment until dinner, and from after dinner until bedtime, I chewed and chewed and chewed.

At school the next morning I told the instructor my dentist's professional advice, saying it gave me the authority to break the rule against chewing gum in class. My teacher stood with his arms folded, looking down at me. He glared at me, wilting my confidence in the dentist's orders. Finally, he shifted his weight, unfolded his arms, put his hands in his pockets, heaved an exasperated sigh and asked, "How many hours are there in a day?"

"Twenty-four," I responded.

"How many hours do you sleep?"

"Eight."

"How many does that leave?"

"Sixteen."

"How many hours are you in school"

"Seven."

"How many hours does that leave?"

"Nine."

"Don't you think," he said, "that chewing gum nine hours a day is just about all that your dentist can expect?"

#441 - WRITE SOME DIALOG

Using the People You Have Known Tool in Appendix #4, write a dialog between yourself and one of the people you listed

- Something that was actually said
- Something that needs to be said
- Something you wish you had said

#442 - APOLOGY

To whom do you want to say "I'm sorry"?

- What did you do or not do that makes you sorry?

- What did you say or not say that makes you sorry?

Did you ever apologize to this person?

- If you did apologize, how was your apology received?
- If you did not apologize, what prevented you from doing so?

Can you now apologize?

#443 - SORRY

When do you feel sorry for yourself?

#444 - MAGIC

Describe a magical moment

What are your magical thoughts?

#445 - UNEXPECTED PLEASURES

Is there something you were never going to do, but when you tried it, found you enjoyed it or were glad you did it?

- Never going to try a particular food
- Never going to have a pedicure or color your hair
- Never going to see the movies of that actor
- You're a dog person and will never have a cat
- Never take that type of vacation
- Never listen to that type of music
- Never read a book by that author
- Never go out with that person
- Never take that kind of job
- Never engage in that sport
- Never have cosmetic surgery
- Or?

What was it about this activity that you thought you would dislike?

What convinced you to finally try it?

- Describe the experience of trying it for the first time

What did you enjoy about this activity?

- Will you do it again?

Shrimp? I would never get close, touch or eat that thing!

by Luna

A long time ago, my husband and I decided to take a road trip from Lima, Peru, to Buenos Aires, Argentina in a VW, camping and surfing along the Pacific Coast. We did not have children and were taking the three months of summer for the trip. The second day of the trip, I started to feel funny, very sleepy and nauseated and tired. My husband said it was too much driving and the heat, and we would take it easier. We spent two days at our next stop walking around town and eating good meals.

The next day we continued toward the Peru-Chile border. We started noticing people along the road offering baskets containing something. We stopped and asked what it was they were selling, and they said it was fresh water shrimp. My husband asked, "Where is the shrimp? I want to see it." I said, "Shrimp?? I am scared of shrimp! They are alive, I hate shrimp and I don't want to see them or take any in the car with me!"

We continued driving despite my husband's arguments to convince me it was safe and the shrimp would not be walking all over me. We decided to find a hotel in town to spend the night because we needed a good rest. As soon as we got to the hotel room, I said, "I want shrimp." My husband said, "It will have to be tomorrow. I am tired and it is a 45 minute drive back to find them, even if they stay this late. And anyway, the hotel kitchen is closed." He went to sleep. I could not sleep. I had never been close to a shrimp, let alone eaten one, but I craved those shrimp like there was no tomorrow.

I jumped in the car and drove back, found them, bought a two pound basket of shrimp and put it in the car with me! I then drove back to the hotel. It was 11:30 p.m. I managed to get the camping stove upstairs, along with the propane tank, a pot, utensils, and a plate. I cleaned the shrimp and started boiling them. I didn't know how to make a dish with them, and did not have any spices or even salt. Besides, I just hated those things!

When I started to smell the aroma, I could not wait, and started eating the shrimp, and found them so delicious! I ate the whole two pound basket! Then I went to sleep like an angel.

The next morning, when I told my husband about the shrimp, he said, "You must be pregnant. It can't be that you now crave shrimp out of the blue." Over breakfast we remembered how tired, sleepy, and nauseated I had been. I went to see a doctor when we arrived in Antofagasta, Chile. I was pregnant!

#446 - FASCINATING

What fascinates you the most about yourself?

#447 - PERSONALITY

What things do you like the most about your personality?

- Do you like your personality better now than when you were younger?

#448 - AURA

What color is your aura?

#449 - SUPERNATURAL

Have you ever seen a ghost?

- Have you ever been haunted by a ghost?

Have you ever had a paranormal experience?

#450 - BREAKING BAD HABITS

How have you broken a bad habit?

- Quit smoking, drinking, drugs, overeating
- Overcome compulsions
- Conquered self-destructive behavior
- Or?

What bad habits have you been unable to break?

- How have you tried to break these bad habits?
- Why do you think you have not been successful?
- Have you made peace with yourself for not being able to break a bad habit?

HELPFUL HINT #48
TAKE SOME PICTURES

Do you feel as though you've run out of ideas and don't know what to write? Take a walk around your neighborhood and use your cell phone to take pictures as you wander. Look at your pictures when you get home, and use them as your inspiration to start writing again.

#451 - STARRING

In the movie of your life, who should play you?

- What would you tell this performer is the key to creating an accurate portrayal of you?
- Where will you permit the performer to take some artistic license in their portrayal of you?

#452 - LOVEABLE

Other than romantic love, how have you been loved?

- By parents, siblings, friends
- By animals

Are you loveable?

- How does it feel to be loved?
- Are you loved now?

Did you ever feel unloved by someone who was "supposed" to love you, e.g. your parent, your sibling, your child, or your spouse?

- How did that make you feel?
- Will this person ever love you?

#453 - HUMAN BEAUTY

Describe the most physically attractive person you've ever met

- Does this person have inner beauty, outer beauty, or both?

How do you feel about yourself when you are around this person?

- Confident - we're all beautiful in some way
- Insecure
- Jealous
- I don't feel any differently about myself than I usually do
- Or?

#454 - CHARMING

Describe the most charming person you've ever met

- What was it about this person that was so charming?

Are you a charming person?

Prince Charming

by Christine Jeston

It was May 27, 1979. I was in my second year at the National Institute of Dramatic Arts in Sydney, and thinking what a beautiful crisp autumn day it was as I rode the bus from Paddington to Kensington. When I walked out of my voice class at NIDA James Belton, a fellow student, ran up and wished me a happy birthday. Surprise! He told me he was going to take me to town to see the Queen for my birthday.

Queen Elizabeth II was opening the Eastern Suburbs Railway that morning. James had always been a Royalist and was proud of it. He was so brave, admitting it without caring what anyone thought. Believe me, there were plenty of people who thought we should have our independence from Britain, and resented Australia footing any royal bills.

James couldn't wait to get started, so we walked down to Anzac Parade to catch a bus to Martin Place where the Queen was going to head after the opening ceremony at Bondi Junction. She was going to walk out of the tunnel and past the post office to George Street and her motorcade. When we got there, only a few people were congregating, so we sat on the ground and chatted until we saw some men starting to put up barricades. We asked a police woman if she knew which side the Queen would be walking down. She told us the left side, so we positioned ourselves and settled in for the wait.

After a long time, a bunch of men in grey suits came out of the tunnel talking on their headphones. We saw the Queen on the other side. We knew it was her because we spied her hat first. Everyone got excited and some people started cheering. I found myself getting caught up in all the hoopla and was very put out because I couldn't get a good look at her. As I was up on my tippy toes and stretching my neck to get a peek, several men on the other side of the railing were blocking my view so I said very loudly, "Would you please get out of the way. I want to see the Queen!" One of the men looked me straight in the eye and said in the most beautiful English accent, "I am terribly sorry, you'll just have to put up with me."

I had to take a breath as I was utterly bowled over by this gentleman's grace and charisma. I had insulted Royalty! He was Prince Phillip, the Duke of Edinburgh. The Queen's better half, but after seeing him I would definitely say he just may be the better half of that union. Wow!

I have never found the Duke to be particularly handsome, but this man had an unmistakable presence. He was so charming. It washed through me before I realized who he was, and I completely forgot about Her Majesty. I looked at James horrified. He said, "Bubby, this is one birthday you'll never forget."

If this had happened two hundred years before, I may have found myself in the Tower of London or shipped off to the colonies. I was already there, but you get my drift. He really had the most captivating smile and sense of humor. I guess you would have to have a sense of humor if you always had to walk behind your wife.

Just what is charisma? You always know if someone possesses it. CocoB my Maltese has it. I have heard the Dali Lama has it, and I am sure George Clooney has it although I have never met him. The Bible says that Jesus had an unmistakable presence. This list is not necessarily in order, although I do think my dog should stay at the top of the list.

Take my word for it, the Duke has it. I have no idea if Liz has it or not as I never had the privilege, but you never know what will happen. I never imagined when I woke up on my 26th birthday in 1979, that by the end of the day I would have insulted Royalty.

#455 - ADULTHOOD

When did you stop calling yourself a boy or a girl and start calling yourself a man or a woman?

What happened to cause this change?

- You went through puberty
- You went to college
- You had sex
- You married
- You bought a house
- You got your first "real" job
- It became silly to call someone your age a boy or a girl
- Or?

If you still call yourself a girl or a boy, what needs to happen for you to feel you've become a woman or a man?

#456 - SEXY YOU

Write an erotic story in which you are the star

#457 - LOOK AT ME

What do you do to attract attention?

- How does being noticed influence the way you feel about yourself?

Do you even want to attract attention?

#458 - BEST PARTY

Describe the best party you ever attended

- What made it the best?
- Who was there?
- What was the reason for the party?
- Were you the host or a guest?

The Pirate Ship

by Joy Karsevar

Imagine a pirate ship ... that is where we were married. My husband to be, Alan Raymond Karsevar, built the pirate ship called "Brigantine Sultana" during his spare time with a group of volunteers in Richmond, California.

Alan and I would exchange our vows on Saturday August 11, 1984 aboard the Brigantine Sultana. Our ceremony was to be under sail from Alameda to San Francisco and back. The ship could only accommodate fifty people, so we limited the invitations for the wedding ceremony to that number. We invited 200 people to the reception which was to follow at the Encinal Yacht Club. Since the Sultana was an authentic replica of an 18th century vessel, we decided to dress up in that century's outfits and pirate attire. Alan and I had our wedding clothes tailor-made, and rented the entourage's outfits from a Berkeley costumer.

Alan's parents, Leonard and Evelyn Karsevar, came from southern California, while my parents, Ricardo and Ofelia Tomacruz flew in from the Philippines. We, together with our parents, were very excited as well as quite nervous and anxious. My mother asked to see my wedding gown and shocked, exclaimed upon seeing it, "This is not a wedding gown, this is a costume!" Nerves were all over the place before the wedding. There were a thousand and one details to attend to. What was most pressing was having to bring the Sultana to Alameda under motor (not sail) from Brisbane where her home port was, two days before the wedding. Transporting the Sultana was a feat on its own. It is amazing we still had the energy to go on with the wedding.

By the grace of God, everything turned out beautifully. I walked down the dock beaming, with my favorite flower bouquet (gardenias), holding on to my Dad. Honestly, I think he could not believe he was giving his daughter away on a pirate ship! Alan looked like a real 18th century captain, and was so excited to see me! All our relatives and close friends were so happy to celebrate the momentous occasion with us. The reverend who officiated could not believe his eyes when he saw the ship, and he enjoyed the ceremony and talked so much during the wedding message that we almost ran out of water to sail on.

We had more than fifty guests for the wedding ceremony, but luckily two other boats joined in with the rest of our guests. At the reception we had 200 guests. Food and drink flowed all day long. Everyone had a blast and no one wanted to go home. The celebration lasted from 9 a.m. to 4 p.m. and at the end everyone wanted to still hang around the ship. The grand finale was a gift from a couple of crew members who dressed in tuxedoes, went up to the crow's nest, and jumped into the water.

What an unforgettable wedding! What a great start to our life together! People talked about our wedding for years!

#459 - NO PARTY

Write about a party you weren't invited to

- Why weren't you invited?

Does it still hurt?

#460 - THINKING

What have you been thinking about lately?

- Where does your mind go when it wanders?

10

HELPFUL HINT #49

YOU MAY NOT BE AS FUNNY AS YOU THINK

Have you ever said something you thought was funny, only to have it fall flat or hurt another person? Just as you need to be careful about what you say, you need to be careful about the *tone* of your writing. You do not want something you think is funny or clever to come across as snide, cruel, or mean spirited. Read your stories out loud to help you hear the *tone* of your writing.

#461 - WISH FOR

What do you wish for?

- Do your wishes often come true?

Was there a time when your wish came true in an unexpected way?

- What happened?

#462 - JACKPOT!

How would you spend the money if you won millions in the lottery?

- Would you invest your money to preserve your wealth or spend freely and live for the moment?

Would you share your winnings?

- With other people
- With charities or institutions

What would you buy?

- A new home
- Travel
- A fancy car
- Plastic surgery
- Influence
- Or?

What financial legacy would you leave if you were wealthy?

- How would this legacy differ from the legacy you are currently able to leave?

Would you try to exercise control over others if you had a lot of money?

Would you exclude anyone or anything from your distribution of wealth?

- Why?

How would this jackpot change the way you live?

Would anything bother you about having a lot of money?

- Previously unknown relatives and friends asking for money
- Feeling unsafe and targeted by unscrupulous people
- People treating you differently or liking you only for your money
- Loss of privacy
- Loss of your sense of safety and security
- Fear that you might develop a greedy or selfish attitude
- Or?

Would your money buy you happiness?

#463 - NO (1)

Describe a time when you said no

#464 - NO (2)

Describe a time when you were told no

HELPFUL HINT #50

RESIST COMPARISONS

As you write, resist the temptation to compare yourself to others. It is self-defeating and can lead to inertia and procrastination. There will always be some writers better than you, just as you are a better writer than some other people.

Your goal is to tell your story. If you give in to the temptation to make comparisons, you may end up discouraged, stop writing, and not tell your story at all.

#465 - ACCEPT YOURSELF

When did you stop comparing yourself to others?

- What happened to make you accept yourself the way you are?

If you have not yet accepted yourself, when will you?

- What needs to happen for you to accept yourself?

#466 - MY TRUTH

No matter what else I know, I know this to be true

#467 - LAZY

I'm lazy. But it's the lazy people who invented the wheel and the bicycle because they didn't like walking or carrying things.

- LECH WALESA -

Are you lazy?

- When are you lazy?
- In what ways are you lazy?

How do you overcome your laziness to accomplish the things you need to do?

#468 - LOVE THIS

Describe the thing you most love to do

- Activity or Sport
- Hobby (knitting, scrapbooking, stamp collecting, arts and crafts, etc.)
- A place you like to go (theater, out to dinner with friends, shopping, movies, to the beach or mountains, etc.)
- Travel
- Watch TV and Netflix
- Go to concerts or other music venues
- Read, take classes, learn new things
- Or?

Why do you love doing this thing?

#469 - TOO MANY

"In my world, I can't have too many of ..."

- You can't have too many of what?

#470 - TATTOO (1)

Do you have a tattoo?

- What is it?
- Where is it?

How old were you when you got your first tattoo?

- Do you have more than one tattoo?

Why did you get a tattoo?

- You like body art
- To create a memorial or help you remember a special event
- You were influenced by friends
- For religious purposes
- You got a temporary or henna tattoo for a special ceremony or occasion

Was it a spur of the moment decision or something you thought about and planned?

- How did your family and friends react to your tattoo?

Do you have any regrets about getting a tattoo?

If you were to get a tattoo today, where would it go and what would it be?

Tattoo

by Pamela Applegate

For several summers, my family and I vacationed in the harbor town of Brookings, Oregon. We had a 40 foot motor home, and children and grandchildren often joined us for the two week respite. I planned daily activities for the grandchildren which I posted on the outside of the motor home door so grandkids could check and see what was on the daily agenda. One of our days was tattoo day, and for it I purchased large and small stick-on tattoos of all varieties. Usually our vacation was over the 4th of July, so patriotic tattoos were among the choices. I always placed a flag on my left ankle and one over my heart. The girls were much more decorative, and placed their flags on their cheeks and hands. I often thought I would like to have a flag permanently placed on my ankle, but my husband made it very clear he would not approve. "No tattoos!" he growled one day when I mentioned my idea.

Fast forward to several years later. Still wanting a tattoo, I began researching designs that I would like in keeping with my patriotic heart. My dad and my first love were both in the Navy and I lived on a boat, a 55 foot Chris Craft Constellation. My custom design started with an anchor and a rope, which wrapped around a cross. A red, white, blue, and yellow ribbon draped over the top. This symbolized so much: my dad, my lost love, my faith, and of course the flag. Yellow was for remembrance. The rope entwined in the cross representing "anchored in Christ". This would be my tattoo, not sure when but in the future. I sent my ideas to the tattoo artist five hours away and told her I would be coming soon, just not sure when, and she replied she would try to fit me in.

In 2009 the day came when it was apparent I needed to abandon ship. My marriage had fallen apart and it seemed the perfect time to get a tattoo. A new life and a new beginning with an old love, my first love. I called Bombshell Tattoos and made the appointment. The tattoo artist printed out the ink drawing for my approval and applied it to my left ankle. I loved it. "Go for it," I enthusiastically blurted out.

"OK," she grinned, and started work immediately. Vanessa offered to stop if I needed a break, but no breaks were needed. The adrenalin flowing, I was ready to start my new life represented by my new tattoo. I told her the story of young love found again. The love of a seventeen year old girl and a sailor boy. "Oh," she commented, "let's add the number 17 and I'll fill it in with red ink to symbolize love." I quickly agreed. I felt like I was seventeen all over again, and at sixty that is quite an accomplishment.

Everyone told me that once you have one tattoo you will always want another. And so it was in 2014 that I again contacted Vanessa, but this time in tears. I asked her if there was any way she could squeeze me and my oldest daughter in for a small tattoo each. I tearfully explained the urgency of this tattoo. My youngest daughter had died unexpectedly, and we wanted to memorialize her passing the day before her service.

Vanessa was booked solid, but said if she had any cancelations she would text me. She texted me the following day when we were down the street from her shop. "I'll be there in five," I told her. I explained my youngest's middle name was JOY, and I thought that I wanted a halo over the J, and Vanessa took it from there. In minutes she had a wonderful drawing ready to apply. Mine over my heart above my left breast where I could keep her close to me. My daughter had her tattoo placed on her ankle. Vanessa and her daughter got right to work and both tattoos were complete in less than 30 minutes. The pain of the tattoo was over-ridden by the pain in my breaking heart. Tears rolled down all our faces as the work progressed. The joy my daughter brought to our lives forever etched in a tattoo.

In 2015 I lost my sailor boy to cancer, and still another loss in 2016. I imagine a new tattoo is on the horizon. A feather with birds escaping from the side, which reads "your wings were ready but my heart was not." I pause for now, waiting to see if this will be the next expression of love and pain, not only forever inscribed in my heart but also on my skin.

#471 - TATTOO (2)

Life tattoos you. As you live and grow your body changes. You develop and mature, acquire scars, and finally the tattoos of old age.

Write about one of life's tattoos

- Deepening voice and growing body hair as you mature
- Developing sexual characteristics
- Stretch marks
- Scars
- Wrinkles and sagging skin
- Your first gray hair
- Your old hands
- A limp, stiffness, or other limitations to mobility
- Menopause
- Hair loss
- Or?

How did you feel about this "tattoo" when it was first acquired?

- How do you feel about it now?

If you dislike your "tattoo", did you do anything to change it?

- Surgery
- Changing the way you dress
- Make-up and hair color
- An exercise or diet program
- Or?

#472 - HAPPY

Are you happy right now?

- What makes you happy?

Are you a happy person?

- Do you look forward to each day with anticipation and happiness?

#473 - FORWARD

What keeps you looking forward with hope and anticipation?

- Graduation
- Beginning your career
- Marriage and family
- Retirement
- Travel
- New relationships
- New homes
- Spending more time with family and friends
- New career opportunities
- New education opportunities
- And?

What prevents you from looking forward with hope and anticipation?

- Fear of the unknown
- Money worries
- Worries about work and career
- Fear that you won't find love or have children
- Intense competition in school or career
- Concerns about your physical and mental health
- Loneliness
- End of life issues
- Unresolved issues and estrangements
- Anxiety about your family's wellbeing
- Or?

#474 - GENEROSITY

Who has surprised you with his or her unexpected generosity?

- How did this act of generosity make you feel?

When did you surprise someone with your own act of unexpected generosity?

- What did you do?
- How did this person react to your generosity?

HELPFUL HINT #51

USE PHOTOGRAPHS

Photographs can help you get started. Take out your old photos and start asking questions.

- Who is in this picture?
- Where was it taken?
- When was it taken? If you can't remember the exact date, try to narrow down the time period. Were you in school? Do you remember where you were living at the time? Is there something about the picture that can help date it, e.g. "That was taken in Boston, and I visited Boston when I was in high school."
- What is the story of the picture? What are the people doing?

If you include photos with your memoir, be sure they are captioned with the complete first and last names of all people pictured. Also write the names of the people pictured and the date and place the picture was taken on the back of the photo itself. People well known to you and your children may be unidentifiable strangers to future generations.

#475 - BEFORE

What things do you want to do before you die or are physically incapable?

- A physical challenge, e.g. climb a mountain or run a marathon
- Travel to a certain place
- Something you are afraid of doing, e.g. ride a horse, parachute, speak in public
- Something you wish you had done when you were younger

- Mend relationships
- Get in touch with someone from your past
- Find love
- Or?

#476 - AGING

As you grow older, what things have you done for the last time?

- Wear pantyhose, Spanx, and heels
- Wear a suit
- Write a paper or take a test
- Take extended trips
- Have sex
- Own a pet
- Be in love or in a relationship
- Participate in a sport you once enjoyed
- Or?

Why will you no longer do these things?

- "I'm retired and I don't have to"
- Mobility or strength issues
- Fear of being hurt or injured
- Loss of interest in the things you once did
- "I'm too old; that stuff is just for kids"
- Or?

"What do you mean I'm too old - I still do these things!!"

#477 - YOU AS A GRANDPARENT

Use this exercise to write about your grandchildren and great-grandchildren.

What do your grandchildren call you?

- Oma
- Granny
- Gramps
- Nana

- Grandma or Grandpa
- Abba
- GG (for Great-Grand)
- Or?

What are the names of your grandchildren?

Who are the parents of your grandchildren?

- Do any of your grandchildren resemble you?

Write about the birth of each of your grandchildren

- How you heard about the pregnancy
- How you heard about the birth
- The first time you saw and the first time you held each of your grandchildren

When do you see your grandchildren?

- Regularly because they live with you, visit often, or you babysit
- Holidays and other special occasions
- Weekly visits
- At worship services
- At family reunions
- Not often because they live too far away
- Not often due to an estrangement
- Not often because they are adults and busy with their own lives

Describe the special things you do with your grandchildren

- How has the relationship with your grandchildren changed as they've aged?
- How has the relationship with your grandchildren changed as you've aged?

What treasures of yours do you plan to give to your grandchildren?

- Describe the item
- Why was this particular item chosen for that grandchild?

478 - DEAR NEWCOMER

Write a letter to the newest member of your family

- This could be a new baby, a new in-law, a newly adopted or foster child, a pet, or a person who is like a member of your family

What are your words of welcome?

- What advice and observations about your family do you want to share?

HELPFUL HINT #52

ORGANIZATION

Start organizing your memoir by using a three ring binder to arrange your stories. By using a binder, you can try different ways of organization before you go to the expense of binding and printing your memoir. You can also keep adding to your stories without limit, rather than paying for a second volume if you rush into print too quickly.

Include with your binder clear plastic envelopes so you can add pictures to illustrate your stories. You can find plastic envelopes pre-punched with holes for three ring binders at any office supply store.

See Appendix #5 for additional advice on organization.

#479 - INVENTION

What would you invent to make the world a better place?

- A tool
- A means of travel
- A technological device or app
- A system of government
- A philosophy or religion
- Or?

What would you invent to make your own life better?

#480 - ADULT DISAPPOINTMENT

Describe a disappointment you experienced as an adult

- You didn't get the job
- You didn't find love
- You didn't have children

- You didn't get the promotion
- You didn't have a friend
- You did not have enough money
- You were not able to have a comfortable retirement
- Conflicts and estrangements remained unresolved
- Or?

How did you deal with your disappointment?

- How does the way you deal with disappointment as an adult differ from the way you dealt with disappointment as a child?

#481 - RULES FOR LIFE

As an adult, you may have things you wish you had done differently or had known when you were younger. Your successes inspire, and your failures provide lessons and warnings. This is your opportunity to share your Rules for Life. These are your secrets for living an effective and fulfilling life.

What are your Rules for Life?

What advice would you offer to others?

- Pitfalls to avoid
- Where to find contentment, success, and happiness
- How to deal with the inevitable disappointments and challenges of life
- How to correct your mistakes and move forward
- How to be true to yourself, your hopes, and your dreams
- How to cope with heartbreak and loss
- And?

What do you wish you had done more often?

- What do you wish you hadn't done?

#482 - DEAR GRAND

Write a letter to your grandchild to be opened when she or he is 40 years old

- What do you hope for your grandchild's life?
- What advice would you give to your aging grandchild about being an adult?

#483 - HEROISM

Living your life with integrity and honesty is heroic. Doing the best you can do every day is heroic.

How are you heroic?

True Heroes
by Ann Hamer

An email came to me a few months ago from my English university. "Nominate our most successful alumnus," it invited. Graduates of this university are presidents and prime ministers, senators and investors and writers and scientists and judges and educators and entrepreneurs. A former friend from my university days served in President Obama's cabinet. Is that success? I usually think so.

A few days after I received this email, I had to go to the lab for a blood test. It's routine for me now, so unless the technician is digging away poking and prodding at my shy and rolling veins, I am not apprehensive. Instead, I wait and I watch. I watch the blue collar workers in flannels and huaraches waiting for their pre-employment drug screens, and I watch the kids there for their pre-school blood harvest. I watch the bitty babies, scared and hurting, not understanding the process or their pain, their fear exacerbated by the tsking and clucking of well meaning adults.

On this particular day, two Filipino men came in, each with a very obviously mentally disabled young man for whom he was caring. The disabled understood the process no better than the babies, but were bigger, stronger, and better able to flee. They didn't understand that the tiny sting was as fleeting as the disposable butterfly needle the tech used. The purple band tightens around the upper arm, thump thump to raise the vein, the kiss of the needle, the blood in the vial, and then it's done. Hold the cotton tight, the tech wraps some tape around your arm, and then you go home.

But not for the disabled men. The caretakers led their charges to the chairs where their blood would be taken. Fumble resisting the band. Fumble resisting the needle. Fumble with the cotton ball. Fumble with the discomfort.

And through it all, these two caretakers were angels. Endless smiles. Gently steering their disabled charges beyond their discomfort and their fear and their confusion. Smiling at me, smiling at the techs and the nurses and the receptionists and the other people waiting to be tested. Smiling and encouraging us all.

I thought about success. At my fancy pants English university these two men would have been considered failures. Schlepping around the disabled? You're not a surgeon or a scholar or a Nobel laureate? What a failure.

And yet ...

They're kind
And gentle
And patient
And understanding
And sweet
Unremittingly sweet
And absolutely excellent and good and committed to what they do.

And that is success.

#484 - SLEEPING

Do you stay up late or go to bed early?

- Are you an early riser or a late riser?
- How have your sleeping habits changed as you've aged?

Did you ever miss an opportunity or important appointment due to your sleeping habits?

#485 - HELPLESS

When do you feel helpless?

#486 - SCENE

Describe a time when you left the scene

HELPFUL HINT #53

ENGAGEMENT

Take a look at the books you love. What kept you reading beyond the first chapter? What engaged you so that you wanted to know more about the characters, whether they were real or fictional?

I recently read two memoirs in which both the authors went to Maine on a voyage of self-discovery. In the first memoir, the author did a lot of, "Ooh - look at the birds, ooh - look at the beavers, ooh - look at the logs." His disengagement from his own life made the story dull and lackluster. The other book, while similar, was interesting and engaging because the author wove the facts *of* her life into thoughts *about* her life, giving me, as the reader, a real sense of who she was.

No one lives their life in one note. You go to many different places and do many different things. In writing your memoirs, it is important to bring in the *entire* experience of being you. Even if you spent a summer alone in Maine discovering yourself, other things would intrude. You can't spend the entire time staring at your belly button. Eventually some thought has to be given to what's for dinner.

You have written a successful memoir when your reader says, "I want to know that person better."

#487 - IMMINENT

Have you ever been near death?

What happened to make you believe that you were facing imminent death?

- Illness
- Injury
- Suicidal thoughts
- Or?

Was this an irrational fear or were you actually near death?

- How were you able to survive?

Did others think you were near death?

- How did they treat you when they thought you were near death?

#488 - UNWELCOME SURPRISE

I didn't think this would happen, but it did

- Foreclosure
- Financial failure
- Job loss
- Unexpected or sudden loss of a parent, spouse, or child
- Troubled or troublesome children
- Catastrophic illness or injury to yourself or another
- Flunking a class or failing a test
- Or?

I expected this to happen, but it never did

- Academic achievement
- Job success
- Marriage and children
- Serenity
- Or?

This is how I dealt with it

An Unwanted New Path

by Lynda Barr

A couple of months after my twin sister Laura and I turned ten in October 1961, our world changed dramatically. My mom passed away from a brain aneurysm after being in the hospital for a week in a coma. Laura and I and our younger brother Mike were taken to our mom's viewing, and I remember all the adults looking very sad, and that some of the women were crying. As Laura, Mike, and I were slowly walking up to the open casket, I remember thinking that Mom was so pretty and it looked like she was just sleeping. I was beginning to have some hope that she'd be OK. A man stepped up behind us and said, "Don't worry, your mom will be back." His words began to encourage me UNTIL Dad flew into a rage and tried to punch the man. We heard Dad's angry words saying, "Don't you ever say that to my kids!!!" Some other men quickly jumped in and restrained Dad, and my next thought was that Mom was never coming back.

We lived with friends while Dad went through the grieving process alone. It felt like we had lost him too, especially when the family we were living with moved to Oregon and we began living in stranger's homes, one after another for the next few months, until our friends in Oregon had us come live with them. Months later, Dad finally came and brought us back home. We had a series of live-in housekeeper-babysitters live with us. Finally one of them worked out, and stayed for the next couple of years. My dad slowly began dating and one of his dates, a very tall, pretty woman named Tina was quickly winning us over with her friendliness and warmth. All three of us felt very close to Tina, and hoped Dad would marry her someday. That changed one night when Tina was visiting. Another woman Dad was seeing called, and he was on the phone with her for over two hours. When Tina realized Dad was talking to another woman, she left and never came back.

A week or so later, Dad brought home Opal, the other woman. From the first moment we saw her we feared her. She sat on the couch as my dad nudged us closer to her, but we knew without a doubt she did not like us. I remember her eyes were icy cold and there was nothing but a forced smile for Dad's sake on her lips. Dad continued dating her, and every time Opal came over, she firmly showed us the correct way to cook and clean, how to dress better, and be silent and absolutely not have any say in anything. When Opal complained numerous times to Dad about us not filling the salt shaker full enough or leaving a small food particle on a dish after it was washed, Dad finally sat us down and said, "I don't know why you guys keep upsetting Opal, but I'm telling you right now, that no matter what, I am marrying her."

Once Dad and Opal were married, we moved into her home in El Sereno, along with Opal's three year old daughter Doreen. Laura and I were 13 and Mike was ten. From day one Opal ran the house with an iron fist, and Dad began working longer and longer hours. All he did when he got home was eat, and sit down with his beer to watch TV. He didn't want to hear our complaints and shut us out of his world. After a few months, Opal convinced Dad to send Mike off to a home for troubled boys in Colorado, where he lived until he enlisted in the Navy.

Laura and I continued to live in Opal's home, and tried to be as invisible as we could to survive her wrath each day. One time she showed us a newspaper article about a step-mom who had killed her step-kids and said "Do you see what a person can be driven to do?"

Once Laura and I graduated from high school in 1969 and started attending college, we ended up meeting and then marrying the first guys who paid us any attention. For Laura, it was a bus driver named Joe, and for me it was a fellow student at East LA College named Dale, who had just gotten out of the Air Force. Laura and Joe had a son when she was 20, and Dale and I had a son when I was 20 and then a daughter when I was 22.

#489 - UNFAIR

Write about a time when you were treated unfairly

- As a child
- As an adult
- Now

#490 - INVISIBLE

Write about a time when you felt invisible

#491 - CANDLE

In her poem, "First Fig", Edna St. Vincent Millay wrote, "My candle burns at both ends; it will not last the night."

Does your candle burn at both ends or just one end?

- Will your candle last the night?
- At which end does your candle burn?

My light's blown out!

#492 - LESSONS (1)

What lessons did you learn from difficult times?

#493 - LESSONS (2)

What lessons did you learn from happy times?

HELPFUL HINT #54

GET UNSTUCK

Writing is easy. You just cross out the wrong words.

- MARK TWAIN -

If you are absolutely stuck, try writing a letter, a thank you note, or a prayer. The important thing is to start writing!!

#494 - LISTEN

Are you heard?

- When do you feel voiceless?

Who listens to you?

- Who doesn't listen to you?

#495 - BUCKET

Your time is limited, so don't waste it living someone else's life.

- STEVE JOBS -

What's on your bucket list?

- As a child
- As a teen
- As a young adult
- Now

Why are these things on your bucket list?

- What makes them important to you?

Have you done the things on your bucket list?

- What was it like to experience these things for the first time?

If you have not yet done the things on your bucket list, do you plan to?

- Yes, they are still important to me
- No, they are no longer important or I no longer have the ability to do them

#496 - RELIEF

"It was such a relief when I no longer had to . . ."

- Did you feel a sense of freedom or release when you no longer had to do this thing?
- Did you also feel sadness and loss?

#497 - CIRCUMSTANCES

How have your circumstances changed as you've aged?

- Graduation
- Entry into the workforce
- Marriage
- Parenthood
- Retirement
- Empty nester
- Divorce
- Income changes
- Caregiver for a spouse, parent, or sibling
- Death of a spouse, parent, or sibling
- Grandparent vs. parent
- And?

How have these changes affected you?

- Do you feel more or less important or valuable due to these changes?

Journal of My New Life
by M.B.

I wanted to do and accomplish so many things when I was young and I did most. But still, as soon as I retired from the job I had been doing all my life, I took the autobiography class and then registered for a sign language class at Cirrus College.

I went to Cirrus with a friend who took the sign language class to practice, and I took it because I've always wanted to learn one more language. In the class I had an excellent instructor who gave me the confidence to express myself with my hands. She told me that my personality comes on very strong when I'm signing. As an experienced sign language teacher she understands me, but for a novice or my cohorts in class it looks as if I'm signing letters twice. It was fun and challenging at the same time.

I learned something new and it was very hard, but in the end I was able to say a small history with my hands.

#498 - PRAYER

Write a prayer

- To whom do you pray?
- For what do you pray?

Are your prayers answered?

- Are they answered in expected or unexpected ways?

As you look at your life, can you identify times when your prayers were answered, even if it did not feel like it at the time?

- When did you realize that your prayers had been answered?
- What happened to change your perspective about the answer?

#499 - FAITH (1)

Do you believe in God?

- Describe your concept of God and your personal philosophy of faith

If you do not believe in God, do you believe in a higher power?

- Describe your concept of this higher power

Do you believe you have a soul?

- Is your soul immortal?
- Do you believe in an afterlife or reincarnation?

Do you pray?

- To whom do you pray?

How has your concept of God changed as you've aged?

- As a child
- As an adult
- Now

#500 - RELIGION

Do you practice your faith within a traditional religion?

- What religion?
- How does your religion help you develop your faith?

If you do not practice a traditional religion, how do you practice your faith?

- Your concept of a deity or deities
- The influence of nature and animals
- Your moral and ethical code
- And?

#501 - FAITH (2)

Did you once have a faith or belief that you no longer have?

- What caused you to lose your faith?

Were you raised in a religion that you stopped practicing, and later returned to?

- What caused you to stop practicing your religion?
- What caused you to return to your religion later in life?

Did you embrace a new religion rather than returning to the religion you had as a child?

#502 - SPIRITUAL

Describe a profound and deeply meaningful spiritual experience

#503 - SPRINGTIME

For many people spring is a time of new beginnings. Write about spring

Here are some suggestions

- Memories of Easter, Passover, Solstice, Holaka, or other spring celebrations
- Coloring Easter eggs
- Spring break from school
- Melting snow and the "mud" season
- Sowing crops and the birth of farm animals
- Sunshine after winter's darkness
- Daylight Savings Time
- And?

What do you like about spring?

What do you dislike about spring?

11

HELPFUL HINT #55

LISTEN TO OTHERS

If you are in a writers group, memoir writing class, or just chatting with friends, be sure to listen. You only get to know people by truly listening to them and their stories. Pay attention to what is said, rather than rehearsing in your head what *you* will say and how *you* will respond. Not only are other peoples' stories interesting and well worth hearing, their stories may also remind you of stories from your own life. Listening is not only polite - it also helps you remember.

#504 - SAY YES

Write about a time when you said yes

- Did your heart tell you to say yes even though logic told you to say no?
- Were other people telling you to say no?

What happened after you said yes?

- Was the outcome positive or negative?
- Do you have any regrets?

Was there a time when you said no that you now wish you had said yes?

- Why did you say no instead of yes?
- What did you miss as a result of saying no?

#505 - MIRACULOUS

Have you ever experienced a miracle?

- What happened?
- What about this experience made you believe it was miraculous?

What caused this miracle?

- God or other deity
- Guardian angel
- Luck
- Being in the right place at the right time
- There is no explanation

#506 - AFTERLIFE

Describe your beliefs about life after death

- Do you believe in Heaven?
- Hell?

What do you hope or expect will happen after you die?

- You will meet loved ones who predeceased you
- You will be able to communicate with the living
- Nothing will happen; the end is the end
- Or?

Do you believe in reincarnation?

- If you believe in reincarnation, what is your hope for your next life?

#507 - SAYING GOODBYE YOUR WAY (1)

Write your own obituary

- What do you want to say about yourself?
- What do you want people to remember about you?
- What do you want people to forget about you?

What do you hope people will NEVER forget about you?

#508 - SAYING GOODBYE YOUR WAY (2)

Plan your own funeral or memorial service

- Write your own eulogy
- Write or select your own liturgy and prayers
- Select music, readings, scripture

Goodbye Art

by Jeanne Master

with thanks to Beverly Butler

Goodbye Art. I love you.

Many of us remember the events leading up to saying goodbye to our beloved pets. I wish to share a story about Bruce and Art, his loyal golden retriever dog.

Bruce took old Art to the veterinarian toward the end of Art's fifteen year life. The vet said, "There isn't much time left for Art before his suffering will overtake him."

One day when Art was particularly lethargic, Bruce decided that it was time. He put Art in the car and drove to McDonald's for lunch. He bought three hamburgers and then drove to the park. Bruce and his dog enjoyed their last lunch together; two burgers for the old yellow retriever and one for Bruce. Then they took a nice slow walk in the park watching the squirrels scamper around, but unable to run and catch them. They went home for some rest and Bruce made some phone calls.

Bruce called several neighbors who especially loved and befriended Art, and invited them over for ice cream at 3:00. Bruce said, "Would you like to come over and say goodbye to our friendly neighborhood dog Art?" Everyone Bruce invited came.

At 4:30 that day, Bruce kept his appointment with the vet.

Art's last day remains a wonderful memory for Bruce, and hopefully for Art too.

#509 - ANIMALS AND FAITH

Do animals have a place in your concept of faith?

- Do you believe animals have a soul?

Will you meet well-loved pets over the "Rainbow Bridge"?

#510 - DON'T

What don't you believe?

- What happened to cause your disbelief?

#511 - SYMPATHY

Write a sympathy card

- To whom is this card written?
- What happened to this person that makes you want to express your sympathy?

What will you write?

- Often saying *something* is better than saying nothing at all
- Just say you're sorry when you don't know what else to say

Was there ever a time when you didn't send a sympathy card?

- Did you express your sympathy in some other way?
- How do you now feel about not sending a card?

Was there a time when you didn't receive a sympathy card after a loss?

- How did it make you feel?

#512 - SAY

What is it that you just can't seem to say?

- Why can't you say it?

HELPFUL HINT #56

DON'T BE AFRAID OF REWRITING

Writing is a lot of erasing. You can't edit a blank page.

- PENNY GUISINGER -

Imagine yourself packing for a trip. You lay out the clothes you want to take, and then begin ruthlessly pruning so you won't be burdened with carrying the things you don't need. Pretend that you have to carry your words in a suitcase, and then start editing!

It's easy to fall in love with what you write, but don't be afraid of first drafts, second drafts, and even third drafts. Write and rewrite and write again until your story is told in the way you want to tell it. Then you have to let your baby go, and get some feedback from other people. When you read your own work over and over again there will be errors that you just don't see. After drafting and redrafting, you may lose your perspective and be unable to view things objectively. At that point, it's time to ask someone else to read your story so you can get a fresh viewpoint.

#513 - SMARTER

What do you know now that you wish you had known back then?

- If you had known it back then, would it have made a difference?

#514 - FIVE THINGS

What are five key things you'd like to tell someone younger than yourself?

- What are the core lessons and key values you want to share?

#515 - KEY

Your key to happiness is ...

- Everyone's key to happiness is different, so this is *your* key, not *the* key

What advice would you give to others about how and where to find happiness?

#516 - TO FORGET

What are the painful memories that you just can't seem to forget?

- Hurtful treatment by another person
- Hurtful comments by another person
- Death or permanent loss of a person or relationship
- Something hurtful you said or something hurtful you did to another person
- Being left out, forgotten, or ignored
- Or?

If you could free yourself from these memories, what would change?

- How you feel about yourself or another person
- Your attitude toward life
- It would make no difference
- Or?

Since the past cannot be changed, how have you learned to live with your memories?

- Do you need to forgive yourself or others?

#517 - MYSTIC

Describe a mystical or "other-world" experience you've had

Visiting a Shrine

by Ann Hamer

A few weeks ago my friend Joan came for a visit. I dug out a box where I keep some old letters and a few photos to ask her if she wanted copies of the letters she had sent me over the years. In the box were a few things I thought I had lost or thrown away, including an old 35mm plastic film canister with my Holy Mary Mother Virgin dirt. Here's the story.

In 1988 I was attending the University of Oxford in England. After Michaelmas term ended in December, I went to Turkey to visit my friend Victoria who was teaching at the American University in Istanbul. After seeing the sights of Istanbul, we went to Izmir and Kusadasi on the Aegean coast. Near Kusadasi is Ephesus, and near Ephesus is the last house of the Virgin

Mary. Whether or not this house is actually the last house of the Virgin Mary is unknown, since the claim is based on the visions of a 19th century nun. Nevertheless, the house has become a shrine and major tourist attraction. The house is small and ancient, and when I was there in 1988, there was nothing in the house except its dirt floor, the mud ceiling, and a raised dirt-filled stone case that served as an altar. A few candles burned in honor of Mary. If you look at pictures of the house now, there is a large altar to Mary at the entrance, and the outside walls are plastered with messages and prayers from pilgrims. None of this was there in 1988. It wasn't desolate, but it certainly was primitive.

Victoria and I were there on Christmas Eve. Since Turkey is a Muslim country, Christian holidays are not observed, but even so, there was no one there and we had the place all to ourselves. Since we were both a bit sardonic and both had highly irreverent senses of humor, we started making jokes about the house and the shrine and whether or not it really was the last house of the Virgin Mary. The more we joked, the more we egged each other on, and the more we egged each other on, the louder and sillier we got. I know - terrible and disrespect-ful - and on Christmas Eve too! So call me a heathen.

Eventually one of us - I think it was me - said, "If this really is the last house of the Virgin Mary, let's see some proof." The words had barely left my mouth when - and I swear this really happened - a chunk of the ceiling fell off and landed on the floor behind us. I admit we were spooked. We looked at each other. Nervous laughter. "Let's get out of here - fast." We had been caught joking about the Virgin Mary, and like Queen Victoria, she was not amused.

Before we left, I took an empty film canister from my backpack and scooped up the dirt that had fallen from the ceiling. That's now I came to have my Holy Mary Mother Virgin dirt.

I've had it ever since. It used to be that when I opened the canister dust would spiral up, and it did that for years. Probably just because it was so dry, but who knows? I'm not going to tease or question the Virgin Mary anymore - she really doesn't like it.

I've had that canister of dirt since December 24, 1988. Over the years I've thought about throwing it out, but I just can't. So it sits in a box with other half remembered treasures - and the memory of a friend, an amazing trip during a happy time of my life, and that visit to Mary's shrine.

#518 - SCAR

What is the story of one of your scars?

- A physical scar
- An emotional scar

#519 - FORGIVENESS

It's never too late to be what you might have been.

- MARY ANNE EVANS -

Have you taken any actions for which you cannot seem to forgive yourself?

- What did you do?

How can you forgive yourself?

- What will change for you or for others if you can forgive yourself?

How has this inability to forgive yourself impacted your life?

- Does it continue to do so?

#520 - GRIEF

Things have happened in your life that caused you grief

- Death of family and friends
- Job loss or not getting the job of your dreams
- Not getting accepted to the college or university of your dreams
- Substance abuse issues
- Loss of youth
- Doubt
- Death of a pet
- Divorce or loss of a relationship
- Missed opportunities
- Moving
- Financial setbacks

- Loss due to natural disaster, e.g. earthquake, tornado, fire, flood, drought
- Health problems or disability
- War
- And?

Describe your feelings

- Anger
- Sadness
- Loss
- Betrayal
- Forgotten
- Ignored
- Loneliness
- Despair
- Loss of faith
- It's just not fair
- Calm
- Bitterness
- Cruelty
- Resignation and acceptance
- Renewed faith
- Love
- Strength of character
- Resolve
- Or?

Were you able to talk with your family and friends, or did you reject their help?

Did your family or friends ignore or try to minimize your feelings by not letting you talk about your grief?

- How did that make you feel?

Do you need to forgive anyone or anything in order to deal with your grief?

- Who do you need to forgive?
- What do you need to say?
- What do they need to say to you?

Do you need to forgive yourself?

#521 - SAYING GOODBYE TO OTHERS

Write about the death of someone close to you

- Spouse
- Parent
- Child
- Other relative
- Friend
- Teacher
- Or?

How did this person's death affect you?

- What do you miss most about this person?
- How did this person's death change your relationships with other people?

Reflect on the death of someone close to you

- Things you wish you had said
- Things you wish you could ask
- Things you wish the deceased had not said or done to you
- Things you wish you had not said or done to the deceased
- A sense of relief that your loved one is no longer suffering
- Your feelings now that you are no longer a caretaker
- And?

Do you need to forgive this person for dying?

- How do you now wish to say goodbye?

What do you now need to say that wasn't said at the time your loved one died?

- Do you feel angry at a sudden or unexpected death because there was no chance to say goodbye or ask for forgiveness?
- Do you have any feelings of guilt about this person's death?

#522 - QUESTIONS

Do you have questions to ask of someone in heaven?

- What are your questions?
- Who would you ask?

HELPFUL HINT #57

WRITING FOR FUTURE GENERATIONS

You will not be personally known to future generations of your family, so your story may be like fiction to them. To keep those future generations reading, ask yourself what keeps you reading a fiction book? What does the main character or narrator need to do or say in order for you to keep reading? What touches your emotions? Use your knowledge of what engages you as a reader to encourage your readers to care about you and want to read your story.

#523 - LENGTH OF DAYS

Do you find that your days are too short to accomplish all you want to do, or are your days too long to fill?

- What makes your days either too short or too long?

Do you want your days to be filled with activity, or would you rather just "stop and smell the roses"?

#524 - NAMING YOUR LIFE

What title would you give to the story of your life?

In what part of a bookstore or library would your memoir be shelved?

- Fiction and Literature
- History
- Biography and Autobiography
- Fantasy and Science Fiction
- Mystery
- Horror and Gothic
- Romance
- Cooking
- Children's Literature
- Graphic novel
- Drama
- Art
- Travel

- Politics
- Philosophy
- Or?

Just Call Me Baby
by Maria C.

My given name is Maria Socorro. Everyone in grade school through high school called me Socorro, but my family's nickname for me is Baby. To this day my family and close friends still call me Baby.

When we moved to Los Angeles, I used the name Maria, since it is a lot easier to spell and pronounce than Socorro. These days I am also called Mama by my five adorable grandchildren.

My aunt, Tita Abe, once told me that when I was a toddler and had just starting to talk, she asked me my name. My reply was BABY NA MO (spoken in Pampango) which means JUST CALL ME BABY.

It was a simple reply from a toddler. Baby is who I am from my early years and now in my senior years. Since my book is an unpretentious recollection of my life from my toddler years to the present, why not call my book JUST CALL ME BABY. Baby is the name I love and grew up with.

My daughter Mia thinks JUST CALL ME BABY is a cute and catchy title for my book. I certainly agree, so here's my book, JUST CALL ME BABY.

#525 - I KNEW

I knew I was getting older when . . .

#526 - POSTERITY

What do you need to say for posterity?

- I did this ...
- I believe this ...

- I am proud of this ...
- And?

#527 - LIMITED TIME

What would you do if you knew you had a limited time to live?

- Reconcile with family or friends
- Explore your faith
- Take one last trip
- Give away your possessions
- Donate to charity
- Find a home for your pets
- Look for different medical treatment
- Or?

#528 - EVER AFTER

How do you plan to live happily ever after?

#529 - REVISION

If you could rewrite your personal history, what would you have done differently?

- How would doing things differently have changed your life?

HELPFUL HINT #58

HONOR OTHERS

Telling your story gives you a chance to honor others, because your story is also the story of your family and your friends. Telling your story honors others as it honors you.

#530 - NOURISH LIFE

How do you nourish your life?

- What will you do to continue nourishing your life?

#531 - END

Some people find writing their memoir to be both an emotional and cathartic process. You will experience great happiness as you remember past joy and success. You may also experience some sadness and feelings of regret.

Your life is a journey - often happy, but sometimes painful. As you write about any negativity you feel, you find catharsis, and release yourself to tell your story with lightness, humor, and affection.

What impact has writing the story of your life had on you?

APPENDICES

Appendix #1

GUIDELINES FOR CAREGIVERS

Your loved one[2] may be in care for a variety of reasons. You may be caring for an elderly relative. You may be caring for someone who has been diagnosed with a serious illness or a form of dementia. Each situation presents different challenges. If your older loved one is slowing down but is still able to write and communicate, your role is to provide guidance, encouragement, and direction, and together you may be able to work through many of the exercises in *Writing Your Life: The Ultimate Guide to Telling Your Story*. In other cases, your loved one may have a diagnosis or condition that gives you only a limited amount of time to work together to write their memoir.

If you and this person share a past history, don't let *your* memories and *your* emotions influence or alter your loved one's memories. Unless your loved one asks for your thoughts and memories, avoid interjecting your opinions or your interpretations of past events. This is *their* story to tell based on *their* memories, not yours.

Remember, illness and end of life issues are difficult and emotional for both of you, and you do not want the memoir writing project to become burdensome. Find a time for your loved one to work on their memoir, but make it enjoyable. If it becomes too much of a strain for either of you, put it aside and come back to it later.

Getting started

- Your loved one may resist the idea of writing a memoir. Encourage, but don't lecture. Use this book and the tools provided in Appendix #4 to help your loved one tell their story.
- Respect what is being said by honoring requests for privacy and confidentiality. These stories belong to your loved one, and are not yours to share unless you have permission to do so.
- There is no need to respond to prompts or questions that do not apply.
- If your loved one is facing physical or mental difficulties that may limit the time available, first complete the more general exercises such as growing up, school, marriage, and career, before working on more specific topics. If your time is limited, paint with a broad brush the story of your loved one's life.
- Encourage your loved one to make a regular commitment to work on their memoir by setting goals, e.g. a certain number of pages per session or a certain number of hours per week.
- If your loved one is unable to write, try using either computer voice recognition software or recording the stories for transcription at a later date. Unless you are a professional stenographer, avoid

---

2   This guide is designed for all caregivers - both paid professionals and those who care for family or friends without compensation. Rather than refer to this person as "client/loved one", I will use the term "loved one". Caring for another person is very challenging and an act of love, even when done for compensation.

taking dictation from your loved one because you are likely to miss a lot of the details, and the heart of a memoir is in its details.

- You can help your loved one remember by narrowing their focus. For example, suggest, "Tell me about your favorite high school science teacher," rather than "Tell me about your education."
- Your loved one may have faulty memories, distort the truth, or sometimes even lie about events. This is not unusual. You can insert footnotes later for clarification. This is not the time to argue with your loved one about your memory of what happened.
- Unpack the closets and open the boxes of those precious things saved by your loved one. These things were kept for a reason, and now is the time to dig them out and ask your loved one to tell their story.

For the caregiver

You are entitled to feel grief and anger about the physical or mental changes in your loved one and the stress associated with care-giving. Do not be ashamed if you feel

- Anger and sadness
- A sense of loss
- Forgotten or ignored
- Frustrated
- Lack of support or assistance
- Abandoned
- Trapped
- Lonely
- Helpless
- Loss of faith
- Resignation
- Acceptance

These feelings are normal. Care for yourself as you care for your loved one, and if this project gets too emotional or difficult for either of you, put it aside and return to it later.

Appendix #2

GUIDELINES FOR INSTRUCTORS

Use *Writing Your Life: The Ultimate Guide to Telling Your Story* to teach your own memoir writing class, choosing writing prompts that fit your available time and the needs of your students.

When I teach memoir writing, I have an in-class writing exercise in which participants write for ten minutes on an assigned topic. They are also given at-home assignments to work on between class meetings. Participants have the opportunity to read both their in-class writings and their at-home assignments to the rest of the class. See Appendix #3 for samples of in-class writing exercises.

Here are some suggestions for organizing your class

- At the first class, bring in heavy paper or card stock and colored pencils, marking pens, and crayons. Have all class members (including you) create a name placard. Use the placards in every class to get to know each other.
- During the first class, distribute your guidelines and a hand-out with your name and contact information (phone number and email address), dates, time and place of class meetings, and any additional rules you or the facility have, e.g. no eating in class, parking restrictions, impermissible topics, etc.
- Create a roster with the name, address, phone number, and email address of each class member. Distribute the roster to all participants at the last class.
- Bring to each class extra paper and pens for class members who may have forgotten theirs.

Here are the guidelines I distribute at the first class meeting

- Come to class prepared to write. Bring pen, paper, computer, etc.
- We want this to be a comfortable, nonjudgmental, and safe place for you to write and share. All requests for privacy and confidentiality will be respected and honored.
- Suggestions from class members to clarify a story point are welcome. Critical and hurtful comments are not. Remember, memoir writing is about personal experience, and we don't want any harsh critique to create hurt feelings and resentment.
- The assigned topics are meant to help you tell your story. This is not school, and you do not need to respond to all of the questions under each topic.
- Try to complete the weekly at-home assignments to get the most out of your in-class experience.
- Every week you will have the opportunity to share what you write with the rest of the class. You do not have to read in class if you do not want to. Please don't go over your allotted time when it is your turn to share.

As the instructor, you need to accept that you can't make class members do what you want them to do, what you think is best for them, or what you think they should do. Support them in their efforts, give them lots of advice and information, and then let it go. They will create the memoir they want to create, and if they don't want to do a Cast of Characters or tell who's who in photos because people will *always* know who everyone is, so long as you have given them your advice and made the tools available, you have to accept that it is *their* choice. Don't nag. Your job is to help people tell their story in the way they want to tell it. Be at peace with yourself and your class. Anything else is too crazy-making.

Appendix #3

IN-CLASS WRITING EXERCISES

I learned from teaching my classes that there is just not enough time in the ten minutes allowed for in-class writing exercises for participants to remember an important life event and then write about it. I now use the in-class exercises to help class members loosen up, trust themselves, and learn to write freely. The exercises are designed to encourage participants to think creatively and whimsically, and not be panicked by the pressure to remember.

Below are some writing exercises I've used exclusively in class. You may also use some of the more esoteric exercises from *Writing Your Life: The Ultimate Guide to Telling Your Story*. I have used "Drop the Reins", "Mirror", "Cake", "Shipwreck" and "Online" as in-class exercises.

Greeting Cards

Choose a greeting card from the selection brought in by your instructor. The cards are in envelopes so you will not know the subject matter of the card you chose. After all class members have selected a card, open yours and begin writing.

When you open the card, something will occur to you. You may choose to write about the occasion the card honors, or the card may remind you of a special card you once received. You may not like your card, and be envious of the card of another class member. Write about why you are feeling that way. It's possible nothing will come to mind, and if that happens, start writing by describing the card.

The object of the in-class writing exercise is to help you write freely, so when you begin writing, do not censor yourself and do not over-think the exercise.

Note to instructors - Bring in greeting cards covering a variety of topics: birthdays, Mother's and Father's Day, holidays, weddings, thank you, congratulations, birth announcements, sympathy, graduation, etc. These cards do not need to be fancy or expensive. I find cards at library sales, the 99¢ Store, yard sales, and online.

Ten Uses

Write ten uses for a paper clip, oven mitt, shoe, etc.

Pictures

Select a picture from those brought in by the instructor and spend a few minutes writing about it.

- Why did you select this picture?
- What do you like about it?
- What do you dislike about it?
- Does it remind you of an event or time in your life?

Note to Instructors - Bring in pictures cut out of magazines and mounted on colored poster board or construction paper.

Envelopes

Write a couple of paragraphs about your word or phrase. Do not trade with others. If you can't get started, write about how you felt opening the envelope, the word's definition, or what the word looks like. Just start writing.

Let your mind roam freely. A word may have an obvious meaning, but it may also have meanings special only to you. For example, "First love" may mean your first romantic relationship, but it may also mean the first time you saw a place you came to love, the first time you loved a car, a dog, a flower, climbed a mountain, etc.

Note to Instructors - Bring in sealed envelopes containing random words and phrases. I cut words and phrases out of magazines and advertisements. Have each class member select an envelope. Class members should open their envelopes at the same time.

Your Senses

The details make the story.

This exercise helps you learn to engage all of your senses as you write. You draw in your readers and help them more fully understand your experiences if your stories describe everything you sensed. Help your reader re-live with you the taste of that first kiss, the feel and smell of your new baby, or the special scent of a holiday.

Your five senses are sight, taste, hearing, smell, and touch. Some people have a "sixth" sense - some sort of extra sensory perception.

Your instructor has brought in a selection of items designed to engage your senses. Look at them, smell them, and touch them. Listen to the sound the items make. You are welcome to taste and eat the edible items (but not anything else!!)

Browse among the items and then return to your seat and start writing

- What memories were brought to mind by these items?
- Are you reminded of something pleasant or something you dislike?
- Use all your senses to describe these memories so you are not only remembering, you are also re-living and inviting your readers to re-live the experience with you
- If you are stuck and don't know where to begin, start writing by describing the items and use all your senses in the description.

Note to instructors - Bring in items likely to stimulate the senses and evoke memories. Some suggestions are baby powder, pumpkin pie spice, cotton, pictures cut from magazines, rough textured items, bells, soap, music boxes, peppermint, coffee, and chocolate.

Warn your students not to taste something if they are not sure that it is edible. The first time I did this exercise, two people tasted laundry detergent! Clearly mark the containers holding inedible items so your students are not tempted to take a taste.

Learning to Engage Your Senses

Draw a bubble in the middle of a piece of paper. Write a topic in the bubble, and then draw five sensory spokes, one for each sense, radiating from the bubble. The senses are taste, smell, hearing, sight, and touch. List words and short sentences that relate to each sense as it pertains to the topic in the bubble.

For example, if your topic is "picnic", you might write sensory experiences such as the smell of grass, the sounds of kids playing and buzzing insects, the taste of hot dogs and potato salad, and feel of the rough wooden bench on the back of your legs.

Use your words and sentences to write a story.

Historical Events

Where were you

- When John F. Kennedy, Robert F. Kennedy, or Martin Luther King were assassinated
- On D Day
- On December 7, 1941 (Pearl Harbor)
- On the day of the first moon landing (July 20, 1969)
- On VE and VJ Day
- On September 11, 2001 ("9/11" - the attacks on the World Trade Center and the Pentagon)

- When Secretariat won the Triple Crown
- Mass shootings at Columbine, Sandy Hook, Las Vegas, or Marjorie Stoneman Douglas High School
- Any date of historical significance with special meaning for you

Describe how you heard of this event and the impact it had on you.

A, B, C

Go around the class

- Ask the first person to respond to, "A is for _____" (and the person gives a word starting with A)
- Ask the second person to respond to, "B is for _____" (and the person gives a word starting with B)
- Ask the third person to respond to, "C is for _____" (and the person gives a word starting with C)
- Etc.

Have class members write for ten minutes on the word they gave in their response.

Appendix #4

THE TOOLS

THE LIFE BY TENS TOOL

The Life by Tens Tool is divided into ten year increments with one section for each ten years of your life. Fill out the top of each section. For example, if you were born in 1960, Section One would be Ages 0 through 9 (Years 1960-1969), Section Two would be Ages 10 through 19 (Years 1970-1979), and so on.

Jot down your memories for each decade. Do not try to do this chronologically; just note down one or two sentences as you remember. With these few words you will be able to select memories and stories on which you wish to elaborate. When you're stuck and don't know what to write, take a look at your Life By Tens Tool for a place to start.

Keep the Life By Tens Tool in a place where you spend a lot of time so you can jot down your thoughts and memories as they occur to you. Memories can be elusive things, and it is important to make note of them as soon as you can before they once again fade away.

Ages 0 through 9 (Years _____ to _____)

_____

_____

_____

_____

_____

_____

_____

Ages 10 through 19 (Years _____ to _____)

_____

_____

_____

_____

_____

_____

_____

_____

Ages 20 through 29 (Years _____ to _____)

_____

_____

_____

_____

_____

_____

_____

_____

Ages 30 through 39 (Years _____ to _____)

_____

_____

_____

_____

_____

_____

_____

_____

Ages 40 through 49 (Years _____ to _____)

_____

_____

_____

_____

_____

_____

_____

_____

Ages 50 through 59 (Years _____ to _____)

_____

_____

_____

_____

_____

_____

_____

_____

Ages 60 through 69 (Years _____ to _____)

_____

_____

_____

_____

_____

_____

_____

_____

Ages 70 through 79 (Years _____ to _____)

_____

_____

_____

_____

_____

_____

_____

_____

Ages 80 through 89 (Years _____ to _____)

_____

_____

_____

_____

_____

_____

_____

_____

_____

THE FAVORITES TOOL

Listing your favorites may help you remember.

When I was a child, my favorite actress was Hayley Mills. Thinking about Hayley Mills led me to think about going to the movies with my family. When my father took us to the movies we were not allowed to get anything from the snack bar because, "We are here to watch a movie, not eat." Thinking about going to the movies as a child led me to thoughts about going to movies as an adult, and the discovery that my father had come to believe that getting popcorn and soda from the snack bar was a pretty good idea. Remembering one thing from my childhood resulted in a cascade of memories spanning many years.

Remember that sometimes thinking about your **least** favorite things can also trigger memories.

List your favorites (or least favorite) as a child, teen, young adult, now

Actor

_____

_____

_____

Actress

_____

_____

_____

Article of clothing

_____

_____

_____

Birthday dinner

_____

_____

_____

Board Game

_____

_____

_____

Book

_____

_____

_____

Building

_____

_____

_____

Car

_____

_____

_____

Cartoon

_____

_____

_____

CD/Album

_____

_____

_____

Character trait of mine

_____

_____

_____

Character trait of others

_____

_____

_____

Charity

_____

_____

_____

Club

_____

_____

_____

Collectible

_____

_____

_____

Color

_____

_____

_____

Computer app

_____

_____

_____

Computer game

_____

_____

_____

Cooking ingredient

_____

_____

Craft

_____

_____

Day trip

_____

_____

Day dream

_____

_____

Dessert

_____

_____

Drink

_____

_____

_____

Elected position I held

_____

_____

_____

Fantasy

_____

_____

_____

Fictional character

_____

_____

_____

Food

_____

_____

_____

Friend

_____

_____

_____

Funny person

_____

_____

_____

Funny thing

_____

_____

_____

Game

_____

_____

_____

Grade in school

_____

_____

_____

Hobby

_____

_____

_____

Holiday

_____

_____

_____

Holiday decoration

_____

_____

_____

Hymn

_____

_____

_____

Invention

_____

_____

_____

Job I held

_____

_____

_____

Kitchen Utensil

_____

_____

_____

"Knick knack" or curio

_____

_____

_____

Leisure activity

_____

_____

_____

Mode of transportation

_____

_____

_____

Modern convenience

_____

_____

_____

Movie

_____

_____

_____

Music group

_____

_____

_____

Part of my body

_____

_____

_____

Part of my partner's body

_____

_____

_____

Pet

_____

_____

_____

Photo of myself

_____

_____

_____

Photo of another

_____

_____

_____

Photo of an event

_____

_____

_____

Piece of art

_____

_____

_____

Piece of furniture

_____

_____

_____

Piece of jewelry

_____

_____

_____

Place I've lived

_____

_____

_____

Political leader

_____

_____

_____

Possession

_____

_____

_____

Prayer

_____

_____

_____

Presentation I heard

_____

_____

_____

Presentation I made

_____

_____

_____

Recipe of mine

_____

_____

_____

Recipe of another

_____

_____

_____

Religious rite

_____

_____

_____

Restaurant

_____

_____

_____

Road trip

_____

_____

_____

Scenic drive

_____

_____

_____

Scenic view

_____

_____

_____

School subject

_____

_____

_____

Season of the year

_____

_____

_____

Smell

_____

_____

_____

Song

_____

_____

_____

Sound

_____

_____

_____

Sport I play

_____

_____

_____

Sport I watch

_____

_____

_____

Sports team

_____

_____

_____

Stage play or musical

_____

_____

_____

Talent I have

_____

_____

_____

Talent I admire in others

_____

_____

_____

Talent I wish I had

_____

_____

_____

Teacher

_____

_____

_____

Time of day

_____

_____

_____

Tool

_____

_____

_____

Toy

_____

_____

_____

Travel destination

_____

_____

_____

TV series

_____

_____

_____

TV theme song

_____

_____

_____

Vacation

_____

_____

_____

Vacation souvenir

_____

_____

_____

Volunteer position

_____

_____

_____

Wild animal

_____

_____

_____

Work of art

_____

_____

_____

PEOPLE YOU HAVE KNOWN TOOL

Listing the people you have known is a good way to jog your memory. List all the people you can remember who impacted your life and help to tell your story. This list should include not only your friends. People who hurt you or are your enemies are also part of your story. Even thinking about a celebrity may remind you of a personal memory.

SAMPLE

Name: Ruth Jones

Date/Place/Circumstance: 1988/Worcester College; Oxford, England/University friend

Comment: Ruth was a Canadian studying politics. She was President of the graduate students at the same time I was Secretary. We traveled to Prague together during winter break. She returned to Canada after she took her degree. We exchanged letters for a while, but eventually lost touch. I later read in the college bulletin that she died, "suddenly, at home" in 2010.

Name: _____

Date/Place/Circumstance: _____

Comment: _____

_____

_____

_____

Name: _____

Date/Place/Circumstance: _____

Comment: _____

_____

_____

_____

Name: _____

Date/Place/Circumstance: _____

Comment: _____

_____

_____

_____

Name: _____

Date/Place/Circumstance: _____

Comment: _____

_____

_____

_____

Name: _____

Date/Place/Circumstance: _____

Comment: _____

_____

_____

_____

Name: _____

Date/Place/Circumstance: _____

Comment: _____

_____

_____

_____

Name: _____

Date/Place/Circumstance: _____

Comment: _____

_____

_____

_____

Name: _____

Date/Place/Circumstance: _____

Comment: _____

_____

_____

_____

Name: _____

Date/Place/Circumstance: _____

Comment: _____

_____

_____

_____

Name: _____

Date/Place/Circumstance: _____

Comment: _____

_____

_____

_____

Name: _____

Date/Place/Circumstance: _____

Comment: _____

_____

_____

_____

Appendix #5

ORGANIZING YOUR STORY

Try different ways of arranging your stories, for example:

Chronologically, starting with your childhood

By locale - Where you lived as a child, young adult, in middle age, in retirement

By relationships

- Parents and siblings
- Other relatives
- Spouse, children, and grandchildren
- Friends
- Schoolmates
- Work colleagues

Around collections of your letters and journal entries

By milestones and accomplishments

- During your youth
- During your career
- During your retirement

By specific events related to

- Play
- Military service
- Work and career
- Sports and hobbies
- Club memberships and community service
- School, college, university
- A life changing injury or illness
- Vacations and travel
- Marriage and children
- Retirement

By your changing roles

- From dependent child to teenager to independent young adult
- From student to graduate
- From newly married to parenthood
- From parent to empty-nester
- From worker to retiree
- From adult child to caregiver for a parent or other family member

Appendix #6

CAST OF CHARACTERS

Create a Cast of Characters for your memoir. Include all family members mentioned in your stories: parents and siblings, spouses, children, grandchildren and great-grandchildren (biological, adopted, step and half children), maternal and paternal grandparents and great-grandparents, aunts, uncles, cousins, etc.

Include the full names of all your characters - First, middle, and last names, and the maiden names of married women. Include nicknames if they are used in your stories. For example, this is the memoir of Robert Charles Harper, known as "RCH". He refers to his children as Rob, Tom, and Kit, and his mother's sister as "Auntie Mabes". Be sure to include the relationship of each character to you as the narrator.

You may be able to find birth and death records on the internet. If you do not have complete information, leave blanks. Other family members may be able to provide the missing information.

Sample

Memoir of Robert Charles Harper

Robert Charles Harper ("RCH") - Born December 1, 1925 in Chicago, Illinois; died March 1, 2013 in Claremont, California

Lucy Eileen Simpson Harper (RCH's wife) - Born July 3, 1925 in Los Angeles, California

Robert Charles Harper, Jr. ("Rob") (RCH's son) - Born May 2, 1951 in Hermosa Beach, California

Richard Thomas Harper ("Tom") (RCH's son) - Born September 4, 1952 in Hermosa Beach, California

Katherine Anne Harper ("Kit") (RCH's daughter) - Born October 12, 1954 in Hermosa Beach, California

Marian Collins Harper (RCH's daughter-in-law; Rob's wife) - Born October 3, 1954 in Phoenix, Arizona

Edward Thomas Harper ("Tommy") (RCH's grandson; Rob's son) - Born May 1, 1977 in Sacramento, California; died October 1, 1996 in Taos, New Mexico

Melinda Annette Harper ("Mindy") (RCH's granddaughter; Rob's daughter) - Born October 8, 1973 in Fresno, California

Charles Elroy Harper (RCH's father) - Born August 1, 1897 in Oak Park, Illinois; died June 1, 1983 in Newport Beach, California

Millie Elizabeth Bundle Harper (RCH's mother) - Born June 9, 1894 in Grand Rapids, Michigan; died March 8, 1984 in Altadena, California

Wilbur Robert Bundle (RCH's maternal grandfather; Millie's father) - Born June 15, 1866 in London, England; died _____

Sarah Hilgomitt Bundle (RCH's maternal grandmother; Millie's mother) - Born July 4, 1869 in Guernsey County, Ohio; died _____

Mabel Bundle Schott ("Auntie Mabes") (RCH's aunt; Millie's sister) - Born February 10, 1902 in _____ Michigan; died _____ 1986 in Detroit, Michigan

Butch Orville Schott (RCH's first cousin; Mabel's son) - born February 4, 1924 in Monroe, Michigan; died October 1, 1997 in Denver, Coloradoz

Appendix #7

A SHORT GUIDE TO SELF-PUBLISHING

Congratulations!! Your memoir is finished and you want to publish. NOW WHAT?

What is your goal?

To get started, ask what is your goal and what helps you to accomplish this goal?

- What are you trying to communicate?
- Who are your readers?
- What do you want to be your literary legacy?
- Do you want to market and sell your book in a commercial setting or limit its distribution to family and friends?

Generally speaking, you have four options:

- You can print your memoir at home on your own printer and put it in a notebook along with some photos for distribution to your family. This is the least expensive option if you do not want to sell your memoir in a retail setting.
- You can use a "vanity press" such as Shutterfly. You can publish an attractive full color book with photographs using a vanity press, and create a book you are proud to distribute to your family. However, you will not be able to sell a book published by a vanity press on the retail market, and it can be very expensive.
- You can work with a book artist to create a book which is truly a work of art as well as a memoir as a treasure for your family and friends. By working with a book artist, you can create something beautiful that truly captures the vision you have for your memoir.
- Your goal may be to sell your book in the retail marketplace. My book, *Writing Your Life: The Ultimate Guide to Telling Your Story* is for sale in the retail market. It was self-published through Kindle Direct Publishing, Amazon's self-publishing arm. I chose Kindle Direct Publishing because it gives me access to Amazon's world-wide market. There are many other self-publishing and traditional publisher options, and *The International Directory of Little Magazines and Small Presses* can help you explore those options.

Proofreading

No matter what option you select, you MUST have proofreaders. When you read your own work over and over again there will be errors you just do not see, and you will be unable to view your work objectively. Proofreaders will point out your mistakes and give you a fresh perspective. Be open to their feedback. Writing is very personal, but try not to get defensive. Be willing to listen to what you are told without getting offended or hurt.

Your readers need to feel that your book is worth the investment of both their time and their money. Your first page and every subsequent page MUST be compelling. If readers don't like what they read on page one, they will not turn to page two. Your goal is to make every page of your book so engaging your readers feel both excited and eager to continue reading.

- Ask your proofreaders where they were distracted. You need to take out the things that are NOT part of your story.
- Poor grammar, poor word choice, and historical inaccuracy will make your readers distrust you. If your readers distrust you, your book will never get read, and your readers may be unwilling to give you a second chance.
- At least one of your proofreaders should be a subject matter expert to provide feedback on factual and historical accuracy. When you don't know the facts or can't be bothered to check, you come across as lazy and untrustworthy.
- Another proofreader needs to know correct grammar and language usage.
- Pay your proofreaders. You want professional feedback, and payment will ensure that your relationship is a professional one. If you ask friends to be proofreaders, choose friends with the appropriate expertise, treat them like professionals, and pay them.
- Sign a contract with all of your proofreaders, including your friends. It doesn't need to be elaborate and you can draft it yourself. Include how much your proofreader will be paid, what work is expected from the proofreader in exchange for payment, the date for completion, and that your proofreader has no ownership rights in your book or to any royalties or revenue. It you are not comfortable drafting your own contract, consult an attorney.
- Have someone from your target audience read your draft, but also have proofreaders from a broad demographic. The feedback you get from a Millennial will be much different than the feedback you get from a Baby Boomer, and all viewpoints are valuable.

It is imperative that you have proofreaders, but in the end you must take total ownership of your book. Take pride in what you have created.

Your Manuscript and Your Proof

You will not submit a print manuscript to your publisher, but will download an e-version. Your manuscript must be properly formatted or it will not be accepted. If you are unsure how to format your book, you can hire a book designer to help you with both the interior and exterior designs of your book.

You want your cover to stand out. Take a look at your competition. Do the covers of your competitors tend to look alike? They might if authors writing in the same genre are using covers with a similar look to attract the same group of readers. There are numerous websites with photos you can download for free. If you decide to use one of these photos for your cover art, be sure you have permission to use it for commercial purposes. Don't use a photo until you are absolutely sure you have permission to use it.

Use the back cover to sell your book. Do not waste valuable space with an author biography and photo. Put your biography inside the book and save the photo for your website.

Finally the day comes when you receive the first proof, and your book actually looks like a book! The first proof will be an e-proof. If you are producing only an electronic version of your book, you will not receive a print proof. If you are doing a print version of your book, you will receive a print proof after you have reviewed, revised, and resubmitted at least one e-proof. Review the print proof very carefully. You will be surprised by all the mistakes you did not see in the e-proof. Remember you want your book to be as perfect as possible.

Your book's ISBN

The ISBN (International Standard Book Number) is unique to every book. It is required to market your book on Amazon or the retail marketplace, to place your book in a library's collection, and to be included in *Books In Print*. A new ISBN is required for every edition of your book, even if the book's title remains the same.

If you use Kindle Direct Publishing, you will be assigned an ISBN. This ISBN is used to market your book on Amazon and other retail markets, and to place your book in libraries. Your book will be included in Books in Print using this ISBN. If you change publishers and use a publisher other than Kindle Direct Publishing, you will need to acquire a new ISBN, even if the title and text of your book remain the same.

Copyright Protection

Technically, copyright protection exists automatically in an original work once it is fixed in a tangible medium. The copyright holder (the author) can enhance this protection by registering the work with the Copyright Office. Registering the copyright puts the world on notice that your book is an original work, and therefore has copyright protection. See www.copyright.gov for information about copyrighting your book in the United States. If you are copyrighting your book in another country, consult that country's applicable laws.

Read the Contract

No matter how you choose to publish your book, READ THE CONTRACT BEFORE YOU SIGN. You do not want to end up with unanticipated expenses or having to stockpile hundreds of copies of your book. If you have any doubts about the terms of a contract, consult an attorney before signing. You worked hard, and you want to protect both your book and yourself. Don't let your eagerness to get into print make you careless about protecting your work.

Disclaimer

This Short Guide to Self-Publishing is a general outline of the self-publishing process, and is not meant as legal advice. If you have legal questions, consult an attorney with expertise in the appropriate area of law.

Appendix #8

SUGGESTED READING

Guides for Writers

Benedetto, Mary Anne. *7 Easy Steps to Memoir Writing*

Cameron, Julie. *The Artist's Way*

Evanovich, Janet. *How I Write*

Fulton, Len, ed. *The International Directory of Little Magazines and Small Presses*

King, Stephen. *On Writing*

Lamott, Anne. *Bird by Bird*

Poynter, Dan. *Self-Publishing Manual*

Roorbach, Bill. *Writing Life Stories*

San Francisco Writers' Grotto. *642 Things to Write About Me*

Stanek, Lou Willett. *Writing Your Life*

Strunk and White. *Elements of Style*

Truss, Lynne. *Eats, Shoots and Leaves*

Welty, Eudora. *One Writer's Beginnings*

Writer's Market books

Autobiographies and Memoirs

I have read and enjoyed all of these recommended books. I seldom read about military figures or media celebrities, so their stories are not on my list. I have read some popular memoirs that "everyone" has read, but if I did not like them, they are not on my list.

I regularly search my Kindle for out-of-print books. Some of the autobiographies and memoirs I've discovered have become favorites, and are listed below. Do your own Kindle search for out-of-print memoirs and autobiographies you might enjoy.

Adamson, Joy. *Born Free*

Addams, Jane. *Twenty Years at Hull House*

Armstrong, Karen. *Through the Narrow Gate*

Baez, Joan. *Daybreak*

Banks, Elizabeth. *Adventures of an American Girl in Victorian London*

Beer, Edith Hahn. *The Nazi Officer's Wife*

Bly, Nellie. *Around the World in 72 Days*

Bradlee, Ben. *A Good Life*

Brittain, Vera. *Testament of Youth*

Brown, Daniel James. *The Boys in the Boat*

Bryson, Bill. *The Life and Times of the Thunderbolt Kid*

Cheng, Nien. *Life and Death in Shanghai*

Child, Julia. *My Life in France*

Corrigan, Kelly. *The Middle Place*

Dana, Richard Henry. *Two Years Before the Mast*

Day, Clarence. *Life With Father*

Devonshire, Deborah. *Wait for Me*

Didion, Joan. *The Year of Magical Thinking*

Gilbert, Elizabeth. *Eat, Pray, Love*

Gillard, Pierre. *Thirteen Years at the Russian Court*

Graham, Katharine. *Personal History*

Haley, Alex. *The Autobiography of Malcolm X*

Hamilton, Frederick S. *The Days Before Yesterday*

Hargrove, Marion. *See Here Private Hargrove*

Herriot, James. *All Creatures Great and Small*

Kanter, Trudi. *Some Girls, Some Hats and Hitler*

Keller, Helen. *The Story of My Life*

Kimmel, Haven. *A Girl Named Zippy*

Kschessinska, Mathilde. *Dancing in Petersburg*

Laake, Deborah. *Secret Ceremonies*

Larsen, Eric. *In the Garden of the Beasts*

Last, Nella. *Nella Last's War*

Lerner, Jimmy. *You Got Nothing Coming*

Lindbergh, Anne Morrow. *Bring Me a Unicorn*

MacLean, Rory. *Stalin's Nose*

Marie Louise, Princess. *My Memories of Six Reigns*

Marshall, Catherine. *A Man Called Peter*

Mayle, Peter. *A Year in Provence*

McCourt, Frank. *Angela's Ashes*

McManus, Patrick. *The Grasshopper Trap*

Mitford, Jessica. *Hons and Rebels*

Moore, Michael. *Here Comes Trouble*

Mowat, Farley. *Never Cry Wolf*

O'Hara, Kevin. *Last of the Donkey Pilgrims*

O'Neill, Tip. *Man of the House*

Powell, Julie. *Julie and Julia*

Remen, Rachel Naomi. *My Grandfather's Blessings*

Schaller, George. *Year of the Gorilla*

Shulman, Alix Kates. *Drinking the Rain*

Steinbeck, John. *Travels with Charley*

Tarte, Bob. *Enslaved by Ducks*

Thurber, James. *The Years With Ross*

Vanderbilt, Consuelo. *The Glitter and the Gold*

Washington, Pat Beauchamp. *Fanny Goes to War*

INDEX

ACCOMPLISHMENTS

ACTIVITIES

ADVERSITY

AGING

#282 - Destiny
#334 - Growing Into (1)
#336 - Concepts of Old Age
#337 - Aging Body
#338 - Retirement
#339 - New Perspectives
#340 - Changing Perspectives
#341- Different Perspectives
#373 - Setting Goals
#400- Health
#471 - Tattoo (2)
#473 - Forward
#475 - Before
#476 - Aging
#477 - You As a Grandparent
#480 - Adult Disappointment
#484 - Sleeping
#495 - Bucket
#496 - Relief
#497 - Circumstances
#507 - Saying Goodbye Your Way (1)
#508 - Saying Goodbye Your Way (2)
#513 - Smarter
#525 - I Knew
#529 - Revision

ALTERNATIVE BELIEFS

#311 - What's Your Sign
#312 - Superstitious
#422 - Miracles
#499 - Faith (1)
#502 - Spiritual
#509 - Animals and Faith

ANIMALS

#359 - Dog/Cat
#360 - Animals
#361 - Liking Animals
#362 - Fearing Animals

BARR, LYNDA

BEHR, JEANNE

BRAVERY AND HEROISM

CHALLENGES

#19 - Absent Parents

#40 - Reading

#49 - Technology

#103 - Taking the Test

#126 - Frustration

#152 - Loss of Employment

#155 - Adversity

#188 - Refuge

#189 - Disaster

#199 - Shortfall

#250 - Daring Travel

#253 - Less Traveled

#274 - Abandon (2)

#275 - Blindsided

#280 - Once

#286 - Outsider

#287 - Isolation

#317 - Yin/Yang

#338 - Retirement

#355 - Lift and Lean

#379 - Vulnerable

#397 - Necessary

#400 - Health

#413 - Trails

#418 - Fear

#420 - Conquering Fear

#422 - Miracles

#423 - Rise

#464 - No (2)

#480 - Adult Disappointment

#485 - Helpless

#487 - Imminent

#488 - Unwelcome Surprise

#489 - Unfair

#504 - Say Yes

#512 - Say

#518 - Scar

Helpful Hint #31 - Write Out Negativity

Helpful Hint #46 - Keep a Journal Anyway

CHANGE

CHILDHOOD

CLOTHING

CONFLICT

#259 - Trust (2)

CRIME

#378 - Attack
#380 - Crime
#381 - Criminal
#485 - Helpless

DANGER

#43 - Scary
#188 - Refuge
#189 - Disaster
#220 - Sins
#250 - Daring Travel
#274 - Abandon (2)
#283 - Packing (1)
#347 - Risky
#348 - Dangerous
#378 - Attack
#379 - Vulnerable
#380 - Crime
#409 - Protection
#518 - Scar

DANIELS, MICKI

Movin' to California

DEFINING YOURSELF

#14 - Childhood Dreams
#31 - Your Father
#32 - Your Mother
#48 - Your Generation
#124 - Are You
#125 - If You Could
#131 - Conscience
#147 - Ambition
#168 - Curiosity
#173 - Childhood Legacy

DIAZ, BLANCA

Dear Little Sister

DISAPPOINTMENT

#298 - Regret (2)
#304 - Broken Heart
#327 - No Thanks
#349 - Time
#431 - Also Ran
#459 - No Party
#464 - No (2)
#480 - Adult Disappointment
#486 - Scene
#489 - Unfair
#494 - Listen
Helpful Hint #31 - Write Out Negativity

DREAMS

#14 - Childhood Dreams
#59 - Bad Dream
#138 - Dreams
#158 - Dream Job
#190 - Hunger
#204 - Again
#251 - Special Travel
#265 - Inspiration/Perspiration
#282 - Destiny
#299 - Daydream
#345 - Fame
#373 - Setting Goals
#414 - Arrived

EDUCATION

#80 - School Days
#81 - Your Studies
#82 - School Fads
#83 - School Activities
#84 - Favorite School Days
#85 - Trouble at School
#86 - Teachers
#97 - College/University
#98 - College/University Housing
#99 - College/University Activities

#379 - Vulnerable
#421 - Guardian
#422 - Miracles
#466 - My Truth
#498 - Prayer
#499 - Faith (1)
#500 - Religion
#501 - Faith (2)
#502 - Spiritual
#505 - Miraculous
#506 - Afterlife
#507 - Saying Goodbye Your Way (1)
#508 - Saying Goodbye Your Way (2)
#509 - Animals and Faith
#510 - Don't
#517 - Mystic
#522 - Questions
#530 - Nourish Life

FAMILY HISTORY

#9 - Important Picture
#11 - Family Resemblance
#20 - Changing World of Health
#31 - Your Father
#32 - Your Mother
#35 - Siblings
#36 - Birth Certificate
#44 - Your Grandparents
#45 - Family Stories and Legends
#47 - DNA
#51 - Black Sheep
#52 - Family Mysteries
#53 - Oddest
#55 - Old Folks
#56 - Family Strength
#60 - Coming to America
#62 - Language
#63 - History
#79 - Cures

#164 - Traditional Clothing
#217 - Family Feuds
#225 - Heirloom
#226 - Recipe
#227 - Unique (1)
#478 - Dear Newcomer
#482 - Dear Grand
Helpful Hint #35 - Old Letters

FANTASIES

#14 - Childhood Dreams
#251 - Special Travel
#300 - Other People
#305 - Fantasy (1)
#306 - Fantasy (2)
#331 - Wild
#435 - Feather and Fur
#451 - Starring

FAVORITES

#24 - Toys
#37 - Games Kids Play
#39 - Childhood Reading
#57 - Old Clothes
#66 - Holidays
#77 - Favorite Food
#84 - Favorite School Days
#86 - Teachers
#163 - Clothes
#182 - City
#184 - Quote
#197 - Your Senses
#203 - Jewelry
#230 - Moment
#246 - Fun
#251 - Special Travel
#319 - Thanks
#321 - Pleases
#346 - More Love

GETTING STARTED

GIFTS

GOALS

GRANDPARENTS

GRIEF AND SADNESS

GUTIERREZ, ALEXANDRA

The Origin of My Name

HABITS

#229 - Outdoors
#230 - Moment
#246 - Fun
#251 - Special Travel
#285 - Insider
#296 - Worth
#303 - Love in a Box
#315 - Happiness
#316 - Buying Happiness
#321 - Pleases
#334 - Growing Into (1)
#335 - Growing Into (2)
#349 - Time
#364 - Pets
#389 - Better Than
#415 - Lighter
#422 - Miracles
#424 - Precious
#425 - Free Day
#444 - Magic
#445 - Unexpected Pleasures
#458 - Best Party
#472 - Happy
#493 - Lessons (2)
#515 - Key
#528 - Ever After
#530 - Nourish Life

HEALTH

#20 - Changing World of Health
#78 - Childhood Health
#79 - Cures
#379 - Vulnerable
#400 - Health
#401 - Illness
#403 - Treatment
#408 - Life Lesson
#409 - Protection
#487 - Imminent

HEART

HELPFUL HINTS

Helpful Hint #31 - Write Out Negativity
Helpful Hint #32 - You're Not Always The Hero
Helpful Hint #33 - Show Don't Just Tell
Helpful Hint #34 - Remember Thankfulness
Helpful Hint #35 - Old Letters
Helpful Hint #36 - Ambiguity
Helpful Hint #37 - Acknowledge, Atone, Apologize
Helpful Hint #38 - Read
Helpful Hint #39 - Let Your Voice be Heard
Helpful Hint #40 - It's Not All About You
Helpful Hint #41 - Explain Yourself
Helpful Hint #42 - Go To The Source
Helpful Hint #43 - Developing Character
Helpful Hint #44 - Use A Disguise
Helpful Hint #45 - Journals Are Not Memoirs
Helpful Hint #46 - Keep a Journal Anyway
Helpful Hint #47 - Use Dialog
Helpful Hint #48 - Take Some Pictures
Helpful Hint #49 - You May Not Be As Funny As You Think
Helpful Hint #50 - Resist Comparisons
Helpful Hint #51 - Use Photographs
Helpful Hint #52 - Organization
Helpful Hint #53 - Engagement
Helpful Hint #54 - Get Unstuck
Helpful Hint #55 - Listen To Others
Helpful Hint #56 - Don't Be Afraid Of Rewriting
Helpful Hint #57 - Writing for Future Generations
Helpful Hint #58 - Honor Others

HERITAGE

#60 - Coming to America
#61 - Going Back
#62 - Language
#164 - Traditional Clothing
#300 - Other People

HISTORY

#63 - History
#330 - Time Capsule

Appendix #4 - The Tools

KARSEVAR, JOY

How Our Family Survived the War
Life is Full of the Unexpected
The Pirate Ship

KINDNESS AND GENEROSITY

#131 - Conscience
#231 - Charity
#232 - Let Me Help
#233 - Angel
#238 - Compassion
#239 - Kindness
#263 - Teaching
#303 - Love in a Box
#320 - Your Blessings
#328 - Good Deed
#342 - Better (1)
#422 - Miracles
#433 - Activism
#474 - Generosity
#483 - Heroism
#511 - Sympathy
#530 - Nourish Life

LIFE LESSONS

#22 - My Mission
#34 - Parental Advice
#95 - Lessons From Childhood
#131 - Conscience
#134 - Knowing
#167 - Need
#169 - Meaningful
#175 - Past
#176 - Future
#192 - Wrong
#206 - Parental Guidance (1)
#207 - Parental Guidance (2)

LOSS

LOVE

#370 - Gifts of Love
#422 - Miracles
#452 - Loveable

LUCK

#138 - Dreams
#185 - Chance (1)
#186 - Chance (2)
#277 - Answers
#312 - Superstitious
#329 - Luck
#392 - Winning
#422 - Miracles
#462 - Jackpot!!

LUNA

Shrimp? I would never get close, touch or eat that thing!

M.B.

Journal of My New Life

MASTER, JEANNE

A Day at Dodger Stadium
Goodbye Art

MISSED OPPORTUNITIES

#119 - No Love
#192 - Wrong
#282 - Destiny
#286 - Outsider
#317 - Yin/Yang
#385 - Call Back
#419 - Fearful
#512 - Say

MONEY

#23 - Money
#26 - Pocket Money

PARENTING

PARENTS

PEOPLE WHO INFLUENCED YOU

PHYSICAL APPEARANCE

POLITICS

QUOTATIONS

American Red Cross
Azabal, Lilie de Fernandez
Baldwin, James
Calhoun, Eleanor
Churchill, Winston
Country Magazine
Dickens, Charles
Edison, Thomas Alva
Einstein, Albert
Emerson, Ralph Waldo
Erasmus, Desiderius
Evans, Mary Anne
Frost, Robert
Gates, Bill
Guisinger, Penny
Hamer, Lucerne
Hamilton, Frederick Spencer
Hubbard, Elbert Green
Jobs, Steve
Kemp, Harry
Millay, Edna St. Vincent
Orman, Suze
Ouspensky, P.D.
Perlman, Itzhak
Rantz, Joe
Roosevelt, Eleanor
Shakespeare, William
Thoreau, Henry David
Twain, Mark
von Goethe, Johann Wolfgang
Walesa, Lech
Washington, Pat Beauchamp
Wuhl, Robert

REGRETS

#113 - Jealous Love
#116 - Marriage (2)
#132 - Permission

REINHART, AURORA

My Granddad

RINGLE, SALLIE

Loss of Something Treasured
Love Ever After
Taffy

SASINE, DOROTHY TIMM

My Mother

SECOND THOUGHTS

SECRETS

SELF CONCEPT

#202 - Fictional
#205 - Polite
#208 - Babies
#215 - Non-Parenting
#223 - Your Hero
#228 - Unique (2)
#230 - Moment
#231 - Charity
#241 - Hooray for Me
#260 - Explanation
#266 - Mirror
#278 - Artist
#282 - Destiny
#305 - Fantasy (1)
#306 - Fantasy (2)
#333 - Your Decade
#336 - Concepts of Old Age
#345 - Fame
#355 - Lift and Lean
#357 - Default
#365 - Different
#371 - Intelligence
#374 - Buttons
#410 - Half-Glass
#426 - Worry
#429 - Survivor
#437 - Mask
#446 - Fascinating
#447 - Personality
#448 - Aura
#451 - Starring
#454 - Charming
#455 - Adulthood
#457 - Look at Me
#465 - Accept Yourself
#467 - Lazy
#476 - Aging
#483 - Heroism
#490 - Invisible
#491 - Candle

Helpful Hint #3 - Childhood Perspectives
Helpful Hint #19 - Your Own Unique Self
Helpful Hint #20 - Think About Your Future
Helpful Hint #32 - You're Not Always The Hero

SERENDIPITY

#132 - Permission
#133 - Communications
#138 - Dreams
#165 - Charm
#185 - Chance (1)
#186 - Chance (2)
#253 - Less Traveled
#329 - Luck
#350 - Take a Chance
#372 - Tip
#385 - Call Back
#422 - Miracles
#445 - Unexpected Pleasures
#461 - Wish For
#504 - Say Yes

SEX

#130- Sex
#456 - Sexy You

SIBLINGS

#8 - Growing Up
#11 - Family Resemblance
#35 - Siblings
#217 - Family Feuds
#258 - Trust (1)
#259 - Trust (2)

SIMPSON, RUBY

2617 Euclid Place, Minneapolis 12, Minnesota

SPORTS

STORIES

Scrabble
She Made All the Difference
Shrimp? I would never get close, touch or eat that thing!
Taffy
Tattoo
Teeth
Thank You Carol
The First Time I Held a Baby
The Intruder
The Origin of My Name
The Pirate Ship
The Red Shoes
The Simple Black Dress
Third Love
True Heroes
Visiting a Shrine
Writing Workshop: Day One

SUCCESS

#64 - Special Day
#154 - Goals
#174 - Because of You
#230 - Moment
#265 - Inspiration/Perspiration
#277 - Answers
#282 - Destiny
#285 - Insider
#386 - Did It
#392 - Winning
#393 - Accomplishment
#396 - Proud
#423 - Rise
#430 - Elected
#504 - Say Yes

TALENTS AND SKILLS

#49 - Technology
#137 - Compliments
#144 - Talent

VENTURA, ROSEMARY

My Louie

WALLACH, JOAN

Earthquakes

WISHES

WORK AND CAREER

WRITING TIPS

YOUR INFLUENCE ON OTHERS

ABOUT THE AUTHOR

Ann Hamer is retired from a career in healthcare administration. She lives in California where she leads writers support groups, teaches classes in memoir writing and self-publishing, mentors memoir writers, and leads team building workshops. Ann earned degrees from Oregon State University, Loyola Law School, and the University of Oxford.

Visit Ann on Facebook or send an email to AnnH@writingityourway.com

Made in the USA
San Bernardino, CA
15 January 2019